MEDIA BIAS

Other books in the At Issue series:

MEDIA BIAS

Stuart A. Kallen, *Book Editor*

Bruce Glassman, *Vice President*
Bonnie Szumski, *Publisher*
Helen Cothran, *Managing Editor*

San Diego • Detroit • New York • San Francisco • Cleveland
New Haven, Conn. • Waterville, Maine • London • Munich

For more information, contact
Greenhaven Press
27500 Drake Rd.
Farmington Hills, MI 48331-3535
Or you can visit our Internet site at http://www.gale.com

LIBRARY OF CONGRESS CATALOGING-IN-PUBLICATION DATA

Media bias / Stuart A. Kallen, book editor.
    p. cm. — (At issue)
  Includes bibliographical references and index.
  ISBN 0-7377-2410-2 (lib. : alk. paper) — ISBN 0-7377-2411-0 (pbk. : alk. paper)
    1. Journalism—Objectivity—United States. 2. Mass media—Objectivity—United States. I. Kallen, Stuart A. II. At issue (San Diego, Calif.)
  PN4888.O25M43 2004
  302.23'0973—dc22
                                                                    2004040527

Contents

Introduction

The United States is a deeply divided country when it comes to politics. About half of all Americans vote for Democrats, while the other half are aligned with Republicans. This stark political divide was clearly demonstrated in the 2000 presidential election, which was a statistical dead heat. Democrat Al Gore received a greater percentage of the popular vote, while his rival, Republican George W. Bush, was awarded more electoral votes and won the presidency after a prolonged battle in state and federal courts.

During the election and its aftermath, the media were severely criticized. Republicans said the liberal bias of television and newspaper reporters helped Gore nearly win. Democrats charged that a conservative bias on radio talk shows and certain cable news programs led to Bush's victory. In addition, many criticized the media for simply covering the campaign as a horse race, keeping tally of who was ahead and who was behind in the polls while ignoring important issues. Ironically this criticism was amplified by the media itself in the form of newspaper and magazine editorials and commentary on talk shows.

While the 2000 presidential election was especially controversial, the issue of media bias has long been a subject of heated debate. Newspapers, magazines, television, and radio have traditionally played vital roles in America's democratic society, dispensing news and educating the public about politics, religion, and cultural changes in the modern world. Perhaps no other institutions have been given a greater responsibility. The concept of a neutral press that gives measured and evenhanded coverage to all sides of an issue has been a cornerstone of journalism since World War II. As media critic Tim Rutten writes in the *Los Angeles Times*, "Intellectual rigor and emotional self-discipline enable journalists to gather and report facts with an impartiality that—though sometimes imperfect—is good enough to serve the public's interest."

The nature of media has changed drastically in the past several decades, however, and these changes have challenged the long-held concept of an objective and unbiased press. Whereas in the 1960s there were only three television stations throughout the country, today there are dozens of stations on cable TV. Some of these stations are dedicated solely to various aspects of the news, from politics and entertainment to the financial markets. Since the late 1980s, talk radio has become the persistent voice of conservative politics, with more than 20 million listeners across the country tuning in every day. In addition, the Internet has played an expanding role in media affairs. This trend was accelerated in the late 1990s during the Bill Clinton administration when Internet reporters broke scandalous news stories that were later picked up by newspapers, magazines, and television shows.

This growth of what has been called the new media has profoundly changed the way Americans receive political information and, in turn, how they view the media. Today, while millions still get their news from newspapers and the network newscasts on NBC, CBS, and ABC, they also bookmark their favorite news Web sites, watch political news shows on cable, or listen to politically provocative talks shows on the radio. While the traditional media such as newspapers, TV news, and major newsmagazines such as *Time* and *Newsweek* attempt to adhere to standards of political objectivity, many of those on the Internet, cable TV, and talk radio do not.

Liberals and conservatives can both find media to support their opinions, but each side continues to challenge those that do not. As CNN political analyst Bill Schneider says, political activists have "staked out their positions, and now they want the press to take sides too."

Liberals challenge the media for a perceived procorporate and progovernment bias in the way the news is presented. As an example, they point to the March 2003 invasion of Iraq by the United States. During this event, prowar analysts and those expressing the viewpoint of the Bush administration far outnumbered antiwar voices in almost all mainstream media. In addition, questionable assertions that Iraq possessed weapons of mass destruction [WMD] were repeated frequently. As Seth Ackerman writes in *EXTRA!* magazine, "[Much] of the media had been conditioned to believe, almost as an article of faith, that Saddam Hussein's Iraq was bulging with chemical and biological weapons, despite years of United Nations inspections. Reporters dispensed with the formality of applying modifiers like 'alleged' or 'suspected' to Iraq's supposed [WMD] stocks." According to critics, this distorted reporting is just one example of how the media kowtow to government and corporate interests.

Alternately, conservatives see a long-standing liberal bias exhibited by network newscasters such as CBS's Dan Rather and ABC's Peter Jennings. As Tim Graham and Rich Noyes write about Jennings on the Media Research Center Web site: "During the last twenty years, Jennings' liberal tilt has been obvious—the ABC anchorman has pushed for European-style welfare programs, denigrated tax cuts, castigated Republicans as intolerant, scoffed at suggestions that Soviet communism was a threat and pushed the arguments of left-wing antiwar activists during [2003's] successful war to oust Saddam Hussein." This alleged liberal bias is also perceived in the country's largest newspapers and magazines, such as the *Washington Post*, the *New York Times*, and *Newsweek*. These media outlets are seen as supporting gay rights, abortion rights, environmental restrictions on industry, and other issues favored by liberals.

The conservative charges of liberal bias have been loud and steady for the past twenty years, and this drumbeat of criticism is reflected in public attitudes. For example, a recent poll published on the Gallup Organization Web site states:

> Forty-five percent of Americans believe the news media in this country are too liberal, while only 14% say the news media are too conservative. These perceptions of liberal bias have not changed over the last three years. More generally, a little more than half of Americans have a great deal or fair amount of trust in the news media when it comes to reporting the news fully, accurately, and fairly. Trust in the news media has not changed significantly over the last six years.

While some critics debate the influence of liberal or consecutive politics, others point to the corrupting influence of money on the media. These critics believe that the media mainly seek to attract advertisers, which is their main source of profit. To do so, they resort to sensationalistic programming in an attempt to attract the largest audiences, which in turn translates into increased advertising revenue. As the Fairness and Accuracy in the Media (FAIR) Web site explains:

> Profit-driven news organizations are under great pressure to boost ratings by sensationalizing the news: focusing attention on lurid, highly emotional stories, often featuring a bizarre cast of characters and a gripping plot but devoid of significance to most people's lives. . . . [Major] news outlets have become more and more dependent on these kind of tabloid soap operas to keep profits high.

As such, FAIR believes that a political sex scandal or celebrity murder will receive more hours of coverage than an important bill being debated in the Senate that might alter the lives of millions of people.

The effect of money on the media has grown considerably since 1996, when Congress passed the landmark Telecommunications Act. This bill deregulated the media and allowed big corporations to increase and combine their share of the market in almost every form of media. After President Clinton signed the act, a handful of monolithic conglomerates took control of huge portions of the media that were already undergoing unprecedented consolidation. For example, when AOL bought Time Warner in 2001, it took over several movie studios, almost a dozen book publishing companies, and magazines such as *Time, Fortune, People, Sports Illustrated, In Style,* and many others. AOL also bought sports teams such as the Atlanta Braves and a large swath of cable television stations, including Comedy Central, E!, Black Entertainment Television, CNN, and others. AOL/Time Warner, along with the other media giants such as Disney, General Electric, the News Corp, Bertelsmann, and Westinghouse, together own almost all of the commercial media in the United States.

Critics charge that because a handful of corporations control most news outlets, content has become uniform and consistent, with all media covering the same news stories in the same way. Critics also contend that reporters, editors, and producers practice self-censorship. For example, a network news show would probably not do a story on questionable financial practices of its parent company even if millions of stockholders were affected. Michael Kinsley, the founding editor of the Internet magazine *Slate.com,* which is owned by Microsoft, summed up the situation by saying that "Slate will never give Microsoft the skeptical scrutiny it requires as a powerful institution in American society—any more than *Time* will sufficiently scrutinize Time Warner."

Advertisers also exert great control over the media. A 2000 survey by Pew Research Center found that at least one-third of reporters on local news programs said they were pressured to do positive stories about advertisers and avoid negative stories about them.

The issue of media bias will probably never be settled as long as people have diverse opinions. The mainstream media will continue to play the middle between liberal and conservative critics, trying to please advertisers while offending as few audience members as possible. The new media will target specific audiences who want their own political opinions reinforced, often simply and loudly. Those hoping for in-depth explorations of complicated issues will peruse magazines, newspaper articles, and books that are beyond the needs of most consumers. In *At Issue: Media Bias*, these matters are examined from liberal, conservative, and centrist viewpoints. As the authors analyze and compare various aspects of the media dichotomy, it remains clear that this issue will remain a center of contention for the foreseeable future.

1

The Media Have
a Liberal Bias

Pat Buchanan

Pat Buchanan worked as an adviser and speechwriter for presidents
Richard Nixon, Gerald Ford, and Ronald Reagan before running for
president himself in 1991. Buchanan is the author of six books and a
nationally syndicated newspaper column and is cohost of CNN's Crossfire.

Some commentators claim that the media are not liberal as so
many charge but truly conservative. In reality, most newspaper reporters and television news anchors vote reliably for Democratic
candidates. While conservatives have made a few gains on editorial pages and the cable FOX News channel, there are few Republicans in most newsrooms.

"What Liberal Media?" blared the monster headline atop the full-
page ad in *The New York Times*. Its author was Eric Alterman of
The Nation, who has a book out of the same title.

There was a touch of irony in Alterman's choosing the *Times* to place
an ad declaring liberal bias to be a "myth." For that paper has lately been
embroiled in the greatest scandal in its history, the Jayson Blair affair [in
which Blair repeatedly filed false stories and might have been protected by
his editors because he was black. This scandal was] caused by [the *Times'*]
almost blind devotion to liberalism's god of "diversity" in the newsroom.

And, as a judge of bias, Alterman is poorly situated. He is so far left
he considers network anchors Dan Rather [CBS] and Peter Jennings [ABC]
to be conservatives. Moreover, he argues from exceptions to prove his
rules. Because the *Times* endorsed New York Gov. George Pataki over a
hapless black Democratic nominee, Alterman argues, the *Times* is not
really reliably liberal.

A simple standard

If this issue of media bias is to be discussed, there is a need for some standard of left-to-right. Let me suggest a simple one. If [Democrat] Al Gore is

center-left and [Republican] George Bush center-right, one measure of whether a publication is liberal or conservative would be whether it endorsed Gore or Bush [in the 2000 presidential election campaign]—and which party's presidential candidate it almost always endorses. And if being pro-life and in favor of Bush's tax cuts is conservative and being pro-choice and against the Bush tax cuts is liberal, what then constitutes the liberal press?

Answer: All three major networks, PBS, NPR and virtually all major U.S. papers—*Boston Globe, New York Times, Philadelphia Inquirer, Baltimore Sun, Washington Post, Atlanta Constitution, Miami Herald, Chicago Tribune, Denver Post, Los Angeles Times*. While the *Wall Street Journal* editorial page is neo-conservative, *USA Today*—the nation's largest newspaper—is left of center.

Not only are the editorial pages of most major papers liberal, the news staffs are overwhelmingly so.

Not only are the editorial pages of most major papers liberal, the news staffs are overwhelmingly so. At the annual White House correspondents dinners, conservatives are a tiny minority. Opinion surveys of the national press found 80 percent to 90 percent voted for McGovern [in the 1972 presidential race] and Mondale [in 1984], though Nixon and Reagan both carried 49 states. How many celebrity journalists can you name who support [anti-abortion protest group] Operation Rescue?

If the network news anchors are liberal, so, too, are the hosts of the morning shows, Matt Lowry, Katie Couric, Diane Sawyer and Charlie Gibson. The anchors of the Sunday interview shows are Tim Russert, off [former Democratic Senator] Pat Moynihan's staff, and George Stephanopolous, from [Democratic president] Bill Clinton's staff, and Bob Schieffer of CBS, whom no one has ever accused of being a Dixiecrat [conservative Democrat].

Columnists on the right

Alterman does, however, have a valid point about commentators. Following [Vice President] Spiro Agnew's attack on the national press in 1969, most major newspapers—realizing they had lost touch with millions of readers—began creating op-ed pages and opening them up to conservatives. Today, columnists on the right are fully competitive and many are more widely syndicated than their liberal colleagues.

After the breakthrough by conservative columnists came the breakthrough in talk radio. Rush Limbaugh, Sean Hannity, Neil Boortz, Ollie North, Gordon Liddy, Michael Savage, Michael Reagan and other conservatives dominate talk radio, nationally and locally. It is hard to name a liberal who has succeeded in national radio.

Among the magazines of politics and opinion, [the conservative] *National Review, The Weekly Standard, Human Events* and *The American Conservative* have a combined circulation far higher than [the liberal] *The Nation* and *The New Republic*.

In cable TV, Fox News, which is now predominant, tilts toward Bush, but CNN, whose anchors are Judy Woodruff, Wolf Blitzer and Aaron Brown, lists heavily to port [the left].

Conclusion: Big Media remains a fortress of liberalism, but in the populist and democratic media—the op-ed pages, the Internet, cable TV, talk radio—where people have a variety of voices from which to choose—conservatives prevail. With this caveat:

The House of Conservatism is a house divided. Conservatives of to-day are not the [far right] conservatives of yesterday. Many embrace the [interventionist] foreign policy of [President Woodrow] Wilson, the [liberal] trade policy of FDR [President Franklin D. Roosevelt] and the immigration policy of LBJ [President Lyndon B. Johnson]. They have made their peace with Big Government.

Can anyone name a federal agency George W. Bush or his father shut down, or a single federal program they ever abolished [in accordance with true conservative policy]?

Many of today's conservatives would have been called liberals in the 1960s. Indeed, some were liberals then. And their progeny have come to accept foreign aid, the Department of Education, even the National Endowment for the Arts.

They call it compassionate conservatism.

2

Newspapers' Labeling of Politicians Reveals a Liberal Bias

David W. Brady and Jonathan Ma

David W. Brady is a senior fellow at the Hoover Institution and a professor of political science at Stanford University, where Jonathan Ma is a student of economics.

The liberal bias in newspaper articles can be seen in the terms used to identify senators and members of Congress. A study of articles printed in the *New York Times* and the *Washington Post* reveals that Republican representatives are more often identified as conservatives. Meanwhile, Democrats such as Senator Ted Kennedy are rarely identified as liberal although their voting records show them to be so. In addition, conservatives are more often given negative labels such as "combative" and "cantankerous" while liberals are identified with positive terms such as "respected" and "intellectual." This method of identifying representatives in news stories perpetuates the idea that liberals are mainstream and conservatives are extremists.

During Bill Clinton's impeachment trial, [ABC news anchor] Peter Jennings consistently labeled Republican loyalists as "conservatives" or "very determined conservatives." Meanwhile, the ABC News anchor did not refer to Democratic loyalists as "liberals," treating Mr. Clinton's allies, instead, as mainstream lawmakers. So we asked ourselves, was the media's tendency to label particular senators isolated to the Clinton impeachment trial? Or is there a more pernicious generality? After a study of *New York Times* and *Washington Post* articles published between 1990 and 2002, we conclude that the problem is endemic.

We examined every *Times* and *Post* article that contained references to a senator. Specifically, we set out to reveal the treatment of the 10 most liberal and 10 most conservative senators from each congressional session. . . . Using a reliable news database, we deployed a constant search term to uncover when news writers labeled senators conservative or liberal. For five successive congressional sessions during this time period, we documented when *Times* and *Post* reporters directly labeled Republican loyalists "conservatives" and Democratic loyalists "liberals" in their news stories. (We excluded editorials.)

Conservative senators earn "conservative" labels from Times *reporters more often than liberal senators receive "liberal" labels.*

The first finding of our study is consistent with the results found for media stories on institutions such as corporations, Congress or universities, namely, that most of the time the story is straightforward—as in "senators X, Y, and Z visited the European Union Parliament." However, when there were policy issues at stake we found that conservative senators earn "conservative" labels from *Times* reporters more often than liberal senators receive "liberal" labels.

For instance, during the 102nd Congress [1991–1992], the *Times* labeled liberal senators as "liberal" in 3.87% of the stories in which they were mentioned. In contrast, the 10 most conservative senators were identified as "conservative" in 9.03% of the stories in which they were mentioned, nearly three times the rate for liberal senators. Over the course of six congressional sessions, the labeling of conservative senators in the *Washington Post* and *New York Times* occurred at a rate of two, three, four and even five times as often as that of liberal senators. It appears clear that the news media assumes that conservative ideology needs to be identified more often than liberal ideology does.

Liberals in favorable light

The disparity in reporting was not limited to numbers. *Times* reporters often inject comments that present liberals in a more favorable light than conservatives. For instance, during the 102nd Congress, Sen. Tom Harkin of Iowa was described in *Times* stories as "a kindred liberal Democrat from Iowa," a "respected Midwestern liberal," and "a good old-fashioned liberal." Fellow Democrat Sen. Edward M. Kennedy of Massachusetts received neutral, if not benign, identification: "a liberal spokesman," and "the party's old-school liberal." In contrast, *Times* reporters presented conservative senators as belligerent and extreme. During the 102nd Congress, Sen. Jesse Helms was labeled as "the most unyielding conservative," "the unyielding conservative Republican," "the contentious conservative," and "the Republican arch-conservative." During this time period, *Times* reporters made a point to specifically identify Sen. Malcolm Wallop of Wyoming and Sen. Robert C. Smith of New Hampshire as "very conservative," and Sen. Don Nickles of Oklahoma as "one of the most conservative elected officials in America."

We have detected a pattern of editorialized commentary throughout the decade. Liberal senators were granted near-immunity from any disparaging remarks regarding their ideological position: Sen. Harkin is "a liberal intellectual"; Sen. Barbara Boxer of California is "a reliably out-spoken liberal"; Sen. Paul Simon of Illinois is "a respected Midwestern liberal"; Sen. Daniel Patrick Moynihan of New York is "difficult to categorize politically"; Sen. Kennedy is "a liberal icon" and "liberal abortion rights stalwart"; and Sen. Frank R. Lautenberg of New Jersey is a man whose "politics are liberal to moderate."

Sticky Labels

Classification of U.S. senators as liberals or conservatives.

	New York Times		Washington Post	
Congress	% Lib	% Con	% Lib	% Con
102nd	3.87	9.03	2.04	6.00
103rd	3.18	10.80	2.48	7.31
104th	3.08	8.03	1.90	5.40
105th	5.54	11.95	2.13	6.28
106th	3.71	12.73	2.28	5.52
107th	4.43	6.67	3.68	7.21

Sources: David W. Brady and Jonathan Ma

While references to liberal senators in the *Times* evoke a brave defense of the liberal platform (key words: icon and stalwart), the newspaper portrays conservatives as cantankerous lawmakers seeking to push their agenda down America's throat. Descriptions of conservative senators include "unyielding," "hard-line" and "firebrand." A taste of *Times* quotes on conservatives during the period of 1990–2000: Sen. Nickles is "a fierce conservative" and "a rock-ribbed conservative"; Sen. Helms is "perhaps the most tenacious and quarrelsome conservative in the Senate," and with his "right-wing isolationist ideology" he is the "best-known mischief maker." Sen. Jon Kyl of Arizona is "a Republican hard-liner"; Sen. Robert C. Smith is "a granite-hard Republican conservative"; [Texas Sen. Phil] Gramm takes "aggressively conservative stands" and has "touched on many red-meat conservative topics," as "the highly partisan conservative Texan"; Sen. Sam Brownback of Kansas is "hard-core conservative," "considerably more conservative . . . less pragmatic," "hard-line conservative . . . one of [Speaker of the House] Newt Gingrich's foot soldiers," and "a hard-charging conservative"; Sen. Tim Hutchinson of Arkansas is "a staunch conservative"; and Sen. Larry Craig of Idaho is "an arch-conservative."

Republicans labeled as hostile

This labeling pattern was not limited to the *Times*. Liberal and conservative senators also received different treatment from the *Washington Post*. Distinctly liberal senators were described as bipartisan lawmakers and iconic leaders of a noble cause. In the 107th Congress, Sen. Paul Sarbanes of Maryland was described as "one of the more liberal senators but [with] a record of working with Republicans." Sen. Harkin was bathed in bipartisan light: "a prairie populist with a generally liberal record, although he's made a few detours to more conservative positions demanded by his Iowa constituents." Of Carol Moseley-Braun of Illinois, the *Post* said: "Though a liberal at heart, she is more pragmatic than ideological." Other liberals were lionized or cast in soft focus: "Sen. Kennedy is a hero to liberals and a major irritant to conservatives, plus an old-style liberal appeal to conscience"; Sen. Paul Wellstone of Minnesota "was one of the few unabashed liberals left on Capitol Hill and an ebullient liberal"; Sen. Moynihan was "a liberal public intellectual."

In contrast, the *Post* portrayed conservative senators unflatteringly. Republican loyalists were often labeled as hostile and out of the mainstream. In the 107th Congress [2001–2002], Senators Gramm and Nickles were dismissed as a "conservative Texan" and "conservative Oklahoman" respectively. *Post* reporters regarded Sen. Smith as an idiosyncratic conservative, militantly conservative, and a conservative man in a conservative suit from the conservative state of New Hampshire. Other Republicans were characterized as antagonists: Sen. James Inhofe of Oklahoma is "a hard-line GOP conservative"; Sen. Kyl is "a combative conservative"; Sen. Helms is "a cantankerous, deeply conservative chairman," "a Clinton-bashing conservative," "the crusty senator from North Carolina," "the longtime keeper of the conservative flame," and "a conservative curmudgeon."

The newspaper portrays conservatives as cantankerous lawmakers seeking to push their agenda down America's throat.

Our preliminary results for other papers—*USA Today*, the *San Diego Union-Tribune*, the *Los Angeles Times*—reveal similar patterns to those described above. The major exception is *The Wall Street Journal* and even here the labeling of conservatives to liberals is a little less than 2 to 1. The effect of these findings on senators' re-election, fund raising and careers is little understood, but the relationship is complicated. However, one can conclude fairly from this survey that conservative senators, consistently portrayed as spoilers, are ill-served by the political reporting in two of the leading general-interest newspapers of the United States. Liberals, on the other hand, get a free pass. If this is not bias, pray what is?

3

The Media Are Influenced by Conservative Interests

Janine Jackson, Peter Hart, and Rachel Coen

Janine Jackson is program director of FAIR (Fairness and Accuracy in the Media), an organization that tracks corporate and right-wing bias in the media, and a frequent contributor to FAIR's magazine Extra! *Peter Hart is an administrator and director of FAIR. Hart also cohosts the organization's radio show* CounterSpin. *Rachel Coen is the former media analyst and communications coordinator with FAIR and is now a freelance writer.*

In recent years a few media conglomerates have gained nearly total control over most of the nation's newspapers, magazines, and television and radio stations. Impartial investigative journalism has suffered as a result of this concentration of ownership because these companies tightly control news content to promote their conservative corporate interests. Stories favorable to advertisers are promoted while negative news about them is censored or ignored. Media corporations also exhibit blatant self-interest and blur the line between entertainment and news when they promote movies, books, and TV shows in stories posing as news. Perhaps most worrisome is the willingness of the corporate media to accept the statements of government officials at face value. Without a robust press willing to investigate the integrity and honesty of politicians and corporations, Americans are increasingly uninformed about important issues that can influence many aspects of their daily lives.

It would be hard to overstate the impact of news media in shaping public opinion, on issues from healthcare to plans for war. With media such an influence on us, it's crucial that we understand who's influencing media.

FAIR's annual *Fear & Favor* report is an attempt to chart some of the pressures that push and pull mainstream journalists away from their fundamental work of telling the truth and letting the chips fall where they may. These include pressures from advertisers, well aware of their key role in fueling the media business; from media owners, who frequently use their journalistic outlets to draw attention to, or away from, their other corporate interests; and from the state, as the last year [2002] has made especially clear, with the Bush administration doing its best to promote its own spin on events and to tamp down dissent.

While by no means exhaustive, *Fear & Favor* offers specific illustrations of these broad phenomena, in the belief that an understanding of the forces at work and their concrete, day-to-day impact will help media consumers decode the news they get, and recognize what news they do not get, from the corporate press. . . .

In advertisers we trust

In a commercial media system, the advertiser is king. It's even better to be king during a recession, when the sponsors whose dollars media rely on are able to push for better deals: product placement, extensive promotional packages, etc. Outlets looking for corporate support come up with plans of their own that may be lucrative but hardly seem journalistic. . . .

[For example] the *New York Times* has a special fondness for Starbucks. The front page of its April 29 Metro section devoted over 1,300 words, with two big photographs, to chronicling the coffee chain's rapid growth in Manhattan, along with anecdotes about how New Yorkers "love to complain about Starbucks . . . yet they drink Starbucks coffee by the gallon." Part business story, part lifestyle piece, the article presented Starbucks as part of the New York way of life, explaining that "the coffee shops provide an environment for doing homework, writing screenplays, holding business meetings, socializing after work or reading the newspaper."

But not just any newspaper. As the story eventually discloses, the *Times* happens to have a promotional agreement with Starbucks, requiring the chain to sell only the *Times* in its stores, excluding all other national newspapers. In return, the paper promotes Starbucks in national ad campaigns.

> *In a commercial media system, the advertiser is king.*

The agreement calls for ads, not favorable news stories, but readers may be forgiven a little confusion—especially since, just a few weeks later the *Times'* main front page featured another Starbucks celebration. This time it was the company's European rise that was tracked admiringly, and the Viennese who, though many "sniff that their culture has been infected," have nevertheless made Starbucks a "resounding success." One other difference: This time the paper didn't bother disclosing that they have a promotional deal with the company. . . .

Charlie Rose is a correspondent for CBS's *60 Minutes II* and hosts his own talk show on PBS. He also had another job last year: MCing the Coca-Cola shareholders' meeting at Madison Square Garden in New York, where he gushed about the privilege of being associated with "the Coca-Cola family."

CBS policy is that news correspondents may not do commercials or product endorsements, but a network official told the *Washington Post* that the company was "comfortable" with Rose's role at the Coke meeting. For his part, Rose told the *Post* that he saw no ethics problem because, among other things, he was only paid a "minimal" sum for his appearance (as if conflicts of interest only kick in over a certain dollar amount).

In any case, Coca-Cola's agreement to become a leading underwriter of the *Charlie Rose Show* is not minimal; the *Post* reported Coke will be funding the show "to the tune of six or possibly seven figures.". . .

Attentive viewers may have noticed a mug at Rose's elbow sporting what appears to be the distinctive red-and-white Coke logo on one side, and the *Charlie Rose Show* logo on the other. The *Orange County Weekly* reported that "the mystery" of the mug was solved when guest Robin Williams "picked up the cup with the Rose logo facing viewers, then turned it around to expose the Coca-Cola logo." According to the *Weekly*, Rose responded to Williams' maneuver with "nervous chuckling."

Sometimes media favor their advertisers not with a story's content but with its placement. The *Wall Street Journal*'s October 3 [2002] edition carried an ad on page C3 for the Wall Street firm Bear Stearns. On the same page, readers learned from a news report that Bear Stearns had just made a tremendous error—accidentally ordering a sale of $4 billion worth of stock, instead of $4 million. The juxtaposition of that news with an ad hawking the company's ability to "execute complex transactions—flawlessly" was striking, to say the least; such coincidences are not unprecedented, however, and a usual reaction would be for the paper to move the ad to mitigate the problem. But this time, according to a report from thestreet.com, the *Journal* chose to sacrifice the news instead: Later editions of the paper carried the ad in its original place, while the bad news about Bear Stearns had been reduced to a subsection of another story on a different page. . . .

The boss's business

Media owners, whether powerful families, individuals or corporations, seek to influence news content in many ways. Some seem almost quaintly overt, as when *San Francisco Examiner* publisher James Fang reportedly told then-editor David Burgin: "We bought the paper for two reasons, business and politics. I see 5 percent of the stories having to do with what the Fangs need, promoting the Fangs and our interests." (Days after Burgin made clear he defined the editor's role rather differently, he was fired.)

Corporate boasts of "synergy" are less direct but amount to the same thing: owners using media they control to promote their "interests," as when AOL Time Warner's *Time* magazine declared AOL Time Warner's movie *The Two Towers* a resounding hit before it was released. (Cover line: "Good Lord! The Two Towers Is Even Better than the First Movie.") . . .

And journalists who resist pressure from [their bosses]—whether that means a pushy publisher's office or a mega-corporate HQ—face consequences up to and including the loss of their jobs. Readers and viewers may never learn that a reporter was fired or demoted or moved off the beat. Nor will they be aware of the stories that go untold as a result. . . .

In the novel *Divine Secrets of the Ya-Ya Sisterhood*, the main character,

New York playwright Siddalee Walker, is interviewed by the *New York Times*. But in the movie, Siddalee, played by Sandra Bullock, sits down with a reporter from *Time* magazine instead. As the *Washington Post's*, [columnist] Howard Kurtz noted . . . , "The *Time* interview is mentioned repeatedly in the film, and toward the end Bullock is inducted into the sisterhood and presented with a hat bearing a big fat *Time* logo."

Accounting for the change is not only the fact that the movie was from Warner Bros., another AOL Time Warner unit, but that the *New York Times* would not allow the depiction in the film of events that never took place. *Time*, on the other hand, was happy to cooperate. "Product placement is a good thing," *Time* spokesperson Diana Pearson told the *Post*.

Media owners, whether powerful families, individuals or corporations, seek to influence news content in many ways.

Coverage of the Olympics is a perennial case of corporate self-promotion overtaking news judgment. The 2002 Winter Olympics were broadcast on NBC and its affiliated cable channels, and as previous experience would have predicted, *NBC Nightly News* found the event far more newsworthy than other networks (69 minutes of coverage, compared with 30 minutes at ABC and 10 at CBS). According to ADT Research, . . . NBC's *Today* show devoted 544 minutes to the Olympics—more than any other news story for the entire year.

The use of morning news shows, especially, as promotional vehicles for network fare is not restricted to NBC, of course. Noted J. Max Robins, "CBS's *Early Show* provided slavish coverage of *Survivor* (432 minutes) and the low-rated *Amazing Race* (129 minutes)." Some indication of what all that "synergistic" coverage was replacing: The 79 minutes *Good Morning America* devoted to *The Bachelor* was "more time than was spent on the midterm congressional elections." . . .

Powerful players and PR

A powerful individual, lobby or institution need not own a media outlet outright or fuel it with ad dollars in order to exercise influence. Sometimes the pressure comes from a store that sells the media outlet in question, whose disapproval might affect distribution. Or a powerful corporation makes it known that its displeasure with local media might cost a town jobs and resources. . . .

New York Post columnist Neal Travis cited "widespread" rumors that *Time* magazine's original choice for their 2001 person-of-the-year cover was [terrorist] Osama bin Laden—until Wal-Mart intervened. "I'm told by very reliable sources," wrote Travis, that when Wal-Mart executives heard of the bin Laden choice, they "decided to flex their red-white-and-blue muscles" and "told *Time* honchos that if bin Laden was on the cover in any kind of laudatory position, their stores would refuse to stock that edition." (*Time*'s person-of-the-year pick is not necessarily "laudatory"; it's meant to highlight the year's biggest news-maker—as with Adolf Hitler in

1938.) In the end, *Time* featured [New York City mayor] Rudy Giuliani. . . .

Wal-Mart gave contradictory answers when asked for comment; spokesperson Tom Williams told the *Arkansas Democrat-Gazette* that the rumors were untrue, while spokesperson Jay Allen refused to confirm or deny them, saying that "you could read that [silence] as you choose." Allen did, however, acknowledge that "if Osama bin Laden had been on the cover of that magazine, we would not have liked it and would have evaluated how our customers feel before selling it." . . .

Government and other "official" pressure

Like any government rallying a country for war, the Bush administration is engaged in a massive propaganda campaign. That the war is a vaguely defined, open-ended "war on terror" creates holes that images and "messages" must fill. In such circumstances, the press corps have a special duty to maintain independence, to question official pronouncements, and to inform the public as thoroughly as possible about policies being carried out in their name. With some notable exceptions, U.S. corporate media have not taken up the charge, appearing to see their role as supporting the government at the expense of wide debate and fair treatment of dissent.

The press corps have a special duty to maintain independence, to question official pronouncements, and to inform the public as thoroughly as possible.

In January, a few months after the September 11 attacks, NBC's [*Nightly News* anchor] Tom Brokaw got special access to the White House for a news special called "Inside the Real West Wing" (which aired, neatly, just before NBC's fictional *West Wing* drama). Although the presidential schedule was tailored for the taping for maximum PR [public relations] value, Brokaw insisted that the special was "not an infomercial for the White House." Yet he told the *Washington Post* that part of the reason NBC got such extensive access [to the president] was that the administration was "concerned about the public drifting away from the mission of the war," and "this was an opportunity for them to kick-start it, to keep the country refocused." Apparently, Bush agreed: *The Post* reported that at one point during the day, the president remarked that "while he has to keep the country's attention on the war against terrorism, it's also 'part of Mr. Brokaw's job.'" . . .

In his book *Fallout*, *New York Daily News* reporter Juan González recounts the difficulties he encountered at the paper while investigating the environmental consequences of the [September 11, 2001] World Trade Center disaster. While most mainstream media were uncritically repeating the assurances of officials [that there was no health danger from the massive clouds of dust created when the buildings fell], González was breaking stories about toxins in lower Manhattan that far exceeded safety levels. The backlash was intense; complaints about González came rolling in from one of Rudolph Giuliani's deputy mayors, the head of the New York City Partnership and Chamber of Commerce, and EPA [Environmental Protection Agency] administrator Christine Whitman.

Subsequently, *Daily News* editors "showed a marked reluctance" to pursue the story. "One courageous editor at the *News*, however, refused to buckle under the pressure," writes González. Metropolitan editor Richard T. Pienciak encouraged his reporting and "assigned a special four-person team of reporters to take a closer look" at the health impact in lower Manhattan. But "within days of forming the team," Pienciak "was removed from his post without explanation" and the new team was dissolved. Though Pienciak was not fired, he was essentially demoted from editor to an enterprise reporter for the paper's Sunday edition. [Later, González's information about dangerous pollution was shown to be correct, and it was proven that the EPA purposely minimized the danger to calm public fears.]. . .

The media and the military

An article appearing in the November 10 [2002] *Washington Post* provided readers with a fleeting insight into the real relations between the media and the military. Headlined "War Plan for Iraq Is Ready, Say Officials; Quick Strikes, Huge Force Envisioned by Pentagon," the *Post* report laid out what some government officials considered a likely battle plan for Iraq.

The article relied almost exclusively on White House spin, noting that "the emerging U.S. approach tries to take into account regional sensitivities by attempting to inflict the minimum amount of damage deemed necessary to achieve the U.S. goals in a war."

While the *Post*'s uncritical reliance on the official line is troubling enough, the paper adds this disclaimer: "This article was discussed extensively in recent days with several senior civilian and military Defense Department officials. At their request, several aspects of the plan are being withheld from publication. Those aspects include the timing of certain military actions, the trigger points for other moves, some of the tactics being contemplated and the units that would execute some of the tactics."

The story is almost entirely based on Pentagon officials, so it's hard to imagine their objections. In fact, the propaganda value of the piece is not hidden: One unnamed official comments, "Discussing [the plan's] broad outline would help inform the Arab world that the United States is making a determined effort to avoid attacking the Iraqi people." The *Post* seemed content to provide that platform.

4

The Media Are Biased Against Conservative Economic Policies

Rich Noyes

Rich Noyes is director of media analysis for the Media Research Center, an organization dedicated to combating liberal bias in the media.

Liberals often use bad news about the economy as a way to challenge Republican politicians and their conservative economic policies. The liberal agenda that favors more regulations on business and opposes tax cuts has been aided by television news shows that slant their coverage to the left. A review of the major network and cable news broadcasts demonstrates that television coverage often espouses liberal arguments for greater government intervention. Those who voice conservative arguments for free-market solutions to economic problems are rarely heard.

L iberal politicians have made no secret of the fact that they hope . . . elections revolve around economic issues, including the federal budget deficit, lack of a prescription drug entitlement for senior citizens and . . . corporate accounting scandals. Perhaps one reason for this desire is that liberals watch [network news anchors] Dan Rather, Tom Brokaw and Peter Jennings every night, and they recognize that TV news has framed the discussion of all of these important economic issues in a way that benefits liberals and gives short shrift to conservative arguments.

In the summer of [2002] the Media Research Center reviewed ABC, CBS, CNN, FNC and NBC news programs and Sunday morning interview programs, along with the broadcast network morning news shows. Prime-time magazine shows such as NBC's *Dateline* and discussion programs such as FNC's *The O'Reilly Factor* and CNN's *Larry King Live* were not included.

Our analysts found that coverage of the key economic issues was almost entirely organized around liberal themes and arguments. For instance, liberals blame President Bush's tax cut for the declining budget surplus, while conservatives blame government spending that is rising far faster than economic growth. In their coverage, network reporters aided the liberal cause by focusing almost exclusively on the tax cut, not the problem of rising spending. Balanced coverage would have equally featured both liberal and conservative arguments.

There were rare instances when network reporters deviated from this pattern and offered viewers a balanced perspective or questioned politicians from both the liberal and conservative perspectives. Thus, in addition to documenting the media's prevailing liberal skew, this report will also spotlight those episodes of even-handed reporting, in the hope that journalists will emulate their colleagues' neutral tone. But the presences of occasionally balanced reports does not detract from the damage done by biased and condescending remarks by reporters such as ABC's Terry Moran, who dismissed Bush's 2001 economic program as "a tax cut that was, frankly, cooked up during the heat of a political campaign." Moran made his remark on September 11 [2002], during ABC's commemoration of [the previous] year's terrorist attacks. . . .

Regulations: four out of five networks agree

The big story at the beginning of the summer [2002] was the fiscal health of corporate America. As major companies such as Enron, Global Crossing and WorldCom became embroiled in accounting scandals, network reporters seemed to have just one suggestion: more government regulations. If the President refused to embrace new rules, journalists suggested, it wasn't because he was a principled conservative, but a slave to big business.

"This is a President who has made no bones about the fact that he is not a great fan of regulation, he talks about cooperation, not regulation. Does he have a credibility problem?" CNN's Aaron Brown wondered on the July 8 edition of *NewsNight*. That same evening, CBS's Wyatt Andrews pushed Bush even harder, branding him the "President who, for most of his term, has been 'partner-in-chief' with big business." He didn't mean that as a compliment.

After CBS's Andrews branded the Bush administration a tool of big business, CBS validated their own spin with a poll, reported by John Roberts on the July 17 *Evening News:* "While people are split over whether Mr. Bush is more interested in protecting large corporations or ordinary Americans, there is no question they feel his staff comes down on the side of corporations."

Supporting stronger legislation

When it came to the legislative reaction to [the] accounting scandals, in a span of less than four hours, ABC, CBS, CNN and NBC's reporters all repeated the exact same liberal spin, favorably contrasting the newly-passed Senate bill with the "weaker" House-passed law. On the July 15 *World News Tonight*, ABC's Linda Douglass worried about the effect lobbyists would have on the final bill: "The question now, Peter, is what will happen to this," she told anchor Jennings. "Will it become law? The House passed a much weaker version, and the lobbyists are swarming over Capitol Hill to try to get the House to water down what the Senate has done."

That same night, the *CBS Evening News*'s Bob Orr parroted Douglass:

"The Senate version must be reconciled with the weaker House package. And with some Republicans and the accounting lobby already promising a fight, it's unclear at the moment how tough the final reforms will be."

NBC's Tom Brokaw applauded the Senate vote even as he repeated the same spin of his network counterparts: "Late tonight the Senate passed, 97 to nothing, a bill aimed at shoring up investor confidence by creating harsh new penalties and jail terms for corporate fraud. . . . The Senate version now must be squared with a different, weaker measure that's already been passed by the House of Representatives."

On *NewsNight*, CNN's Brown echoed that the "conference committee [is] set to go to work tomorrow. These things go on pretty much in secret, we will see what comes out of it, but the betting is it will look more like the Senate bill more than the far weaker bill that passed the Republican-controlled House." Not just "weaker," but "far weaker"—in case any viewer missed the point. That night on ABC, CBS, CNN and NBC, there was no debate, zero, about whether the Senate may have gone too far in its regulatory zeal, even though at least one well-respected business correspondent thought that was a real concern.

Only the Fox News Channel managed to report the same development without adjectives or editorially worrying that lobbyists might "water down" a tough Senate bill. On *Special Report with Brit Hume*, White House reporter Jim Angle quoted a remark from Democratic Senator Joseph Biden ("Maybe the President should stop making speeches for a couple of days. He's spoken twice, and the market went down while speaking 500 points"), then added straightforward information about the Senate vote: "People, Biden said, are looking for real things to happen, and that may soon be the case as the Senate passes its bill against corporate fraud, then sits down with the House to negotiate a compromise."

In a telling footnote, after the House and Senate informally settled on a version of the bill, ABC's Douglass acknowledged on the July 24 *World News Tonight* that longer prison terms may not stop corporate crime. After running through the longer penalties for such things as shredding documents and a 25-year prison sentence for a "scheme to defraud," Douglass belatedly admitted: "Still, experts say just the threat of more jail time won't stop corporate crime."

She then ran a sound bite from Columbia Law School Professor John Coffee, who dismissed the congressional action that was widely celebrated just nine days earlier. "It's an election year answer to crime," Coffee retorted. "It sounds good, but it won't affect the sentences really imposed or what prosecutors actually do." It's hard to give ABC credit for finally investigating and publicizing this point of view, since the network didn't present out this contrarian point of view until after the congressional debate was a done deal.

Budget deficits and spending

Network reporters presented the federal budget deficit as a development with negative economic implications. On the August 27 *World News Tonight*, after the Congressional Budget Office (CBO) issued new ten-year predictions about the federal budget, ABC's Betsy Stark decried the deficits. "There is going to be a fairly serious impact if it persists," she prophesied.

"It is already possible to count the costs of a vanished surplus. Seniors may well have to wait for a prescription drug benefit, and what many saw as the nation's best opportunity to shore up Social Security is gone."

That same night on the *CBS Evening News*, John Roberts made it seem as if the CBO had issued policy recommendations alongside its projections: "The Budget Office says federal coffers will not substantially get back into the black unless President Bush's tax cut is allowed to expire as scheduled in the year 2010." Of course, the CBO statisticians did not argue for a return to the Clinton-era tax code, nor did they rule out other mechanisms such as spending restraint as ways to return to balanced budgets. Roberts's artful formulation implied that the "non-partisan" CBO—he made a point of labeling them as such—agreed with liberals that the main problem was the tax cut, not constantly growing spending.

The debate over prescription drug coverage for seniors

Yet network correspondents' concerns about the expanding deficit evaporated when it came to the debate about expanding the amount of money taxpayers would pay to subsidize the prescription drug costs of senior citizens no matter how affluent. On this issue, television focused on telling the stories of cash-strapped individual seniors with sky-high drug bills, not detailing the overall costs of the program or the probability that another entitlement program modeled after Medicare or Medicaid would lead to higher deficits.

NBC's Lisa Myers was typical, beginning her July 31 *Nightly News* piece with an anecdotal victim: "Rosemary Cola takes 19 pills a day for serious chronic conditions, including diabetes. Her husband Jim takes 11. They had hoped that after years of political promises they'd finally get help soon with drug costs of almost $1,000 a month. So today after the Senate rejected a last-ditch compromise and all but gave up for the year, the Colas were furious."

On ABC's *World News Tonight* the previous night, Linda Douglass used the exact same journalistic formula to elicit sympathy for the senior citizens whom the Senate had not aided: "As she watched the debate, Frieda Moss's hopes for prescription drug coverage faded once again. . . . Frieda spends $500 a month on medicine for diabetes, high blood pressure and heart trouble. The drug bills eat up her entire Social Security check. She has little money for anything else. . . . Frieda and millions of others like her may just have to wait, as one proposal after another goes down to defeat in Congress."

Coverage of the key economic issues was almost entirely organized around liberal themes and arguments.

Such stories are designed to stoke emotions, not inform the public. How many senior citizens are in the same straits as Rosemary Cola and Frieda Moss? What percentage face such high drug costs, and what percentage of those need financial assistance? What are the free-market alternatives to a major expansion of a government program? The networks' decision to organize their coverage of the prescription drug debate around a relative handful of sympathetic seniors seems calculated to push taxpayers toward embracing a new federal burden. That's necessary context, of course, but journalists should also have skeptically challenged the advocates of such a big-government expansion to prove their case.

Pushing a tax cut rollback

Television reporters were not as sympathetic toward taxpayers as they were to elderly prescription drug users. Even while correspondents were chastising Congress's failure to spend more money, concern about the rising deficit manifested itself in a renewal of [the previous] year's hostile coverage of the Bush tax cut. . . .

According to the liberal media's economic template, deficit spending is bad because government borrowing forces interest rates to rise, and higher interest rates hurt economic growth. Yet few liberal pundits perceive the harmful anti-growth consequences when [taxes are raised]. Thus, schemes to postpone or even repeal tax cuts [of 2001] featured prominently on the networks' economic news agenda this year.

A sign of just how pervasive the anti-tax cut bias is at the networks: NBC's Tim Russert—normally a balanced interviewer who presses both liberals and conservatives to justify their positions—used his position as moderator of *Meet the Press* to push the idea of either freezing or repealing the Bush tax cut. On his weekly *Meet the Press* since the beginning of 2002, Russert has asked a total of 40 questions about weakening the Bush tax cut and not one about whether taxes are too high.

[John] Roberts never confronted the liberal . . . with conservative arguments; he only wondered why Democrats weren't doing more to undo Bush's tax cut.

As any good interviewer would do, Russert demanded that tax cut supporters such as Treasury Secretary Paul O'Neill, Speaker of the House Dennis Hastert, and Office of Management and Budget Director Mitch Daniels justify their stance in favor of lower taxes. But Russert indulged liberal opponents of the Bush tax cut, pressing them on whether or not they would support a rollback in its provisions. "If the President's tax cut, in your estimation, is driving these deficits, why not step forward and say 'We should end the tax cut, roll it back,'" he demanded of the liberal Senate Budget Chairman Kent Conrad (D-ND) on June 9.

Democratic Representative Nita Lowey, who opposed [the] tax cut, appeared on the September 1 *Meet the Press* alongside Representative Tom Davis of Virginia, a tax-cut supporter. In a five-and-a-half minute span, Russert badgered them both about repealing the tax cut a total of eight times, or about once every 41 seconds.

Here, in compact form, are six of Russert's questions: He started by asking Lowey, "Should the Democrats be in favor of freezing the Bush tax cut?" Then to Davis: "Would it be better to freeze, postpone, the Bush tax cut?" To Lowey: "Why not freeze the tax cut rather than spend the Social Security surplus?" After Lowey remarked that the Republicans had "squandered" the surplus, he probed: "How did they squander it? With the tax cut?" Russert asked Lowey: "As part of a budget summit, would you be in favor of freezing the Bush tax cut?" Then he turned back to Davis: "But, Congressman Davis, you did come to office with a $5.6 trillion surplus, and it's gone, and a third of that can be directly attributed to the tax cut."

Senator Hillary Clinton voted against Bush's tax cut and began lobbying for its demise in 2001, yet on September 15, Russert didn't press her for alternative policies to promote economic growth, but merely allowed her to reaffirm her anti-tax views: "You said we should repeal the Bush tax cut. Do you believe that is now necessary in order to have the money to fight wars?" What a softball—she thought repealing the tax cut was "necessary" *without* the war.

Ignoring the conservative view

Of course, Russert was hardly alone. The same day the *Meet the Press* host was inviting Representative Lowey to bash the tax cut, CBS's John Roberts was substituting for Bob Schieffer on *Face the Nation*, questioning Democratic National Committee Chairman Terry McAuliffe, an ardent foe of Bush's tax cut. Roberts never confronted the liberal McAuliffe with conservative arguments; he only wondered why Democrats weren't doing more to undo Bush's tax cut: "If you're so critical of the President and his handling of the economy and deficits why is there no great hue and cry among Democrats in Congress to repeal the tax cut?" he pleaded.

Roberts's follow-up question was no less obsequious, as he repeated Democratic talking points to the man who helped write them: "Is now the time for the President to be proposing new tax cuts, particularly ones that seem to benefit wealthy investors more than they do middle- and lower-income Americans?" When McAuliffe proceeded to, predictably, malign the tax cuts, Roberts returned to his original theme: "So why, and I asked you this before, why no hue and cry to roll back the current tax cut?"

Even if interviewers like Russert and Roberts repeatedly bring up rolling back the tax cut as a way to get Democratic politicians to put their money where their mouth is, such a steady drumbeat only reinforces the liberal point that lower taxes are harmful. If, in an alternate universe, both liberal and conservative politicians were asked over and over again about cutting taxes, liberals might quite rightly feel that their point of view was being de-legitimized. In the real world, however, the liberal view is usually well-represented in the agenda and premise of journalists' questions; it's the conservative view that's routinely ignored.

5

The Corporate Media Threaten Democracy

Robert W. McChesney and John Nichols

Robert W. McChesney has written several books on the mass media and democracy and is a research professor at the Institute of Communications Research and the Graduate School of Library and Information Science at the University of Illinois at Urbana-Champaign. John Nichols is Washington correspondent to the Nation *and the recipient of the Clarion Award for newspaper column writing.*

Every day, media consumers are titillated, terrified, and manipulated by reports of celebrity sex scandals, brutal murders, and other engaging news known as "infotainment." Important political issues concerning the American public, however, are ignored or marginalized. Instead of investigating the honesty of politicians, news sources often parrot government pronouncements in order to curry favor with officials who have the power to regulate the media. This media bias benefits the wealthy few at the expense of the majority and is dangerous for American democracy. Unless the public takes back control of the media, people will continue to make decisions in ignorance, based on propaganda put forth by politicians and the media corporations.

It is imperative for Americans who care about democracy to come together and organize a mass movement for reform of the media system.

Two core observations bring us to this conclusion. The first is that the current media system is the direct result of explicit government policies, and that these policies have been made in a corrupt manner with minimal public participation. On this point there is virtually no debate.

Our second observation is that the existing media system in the United States operates in a manner that is highly detrimental to the requirements of a democratic and self-governing society. The system works to advance the interests of the wealthy few, rather than the many. This is a much more controversial argument, if only because it is an extraordinarily sensitive matter, going directly to the heart of how power operates in our society.

Yet . . . the case against the U.S. media system as it currently operates forms an overwhelming indictment.

Americans devour media at a staggering rate; in 2002, the average American spent almost twelve hours per day with some form of media. We are also in the midst of an unprecedented technological revolution—based around digital technologies, typified by the Internet—that looks to weave media and electronic communication into nearly every waking moment of our lives. In conventional parlance, these developments are presented as benign; they are, we are told, all about liberating individuals, investors, and consumers from the constraints of time and space while offering a cornucopia of exciting new options and possibilities. This, however, is a superficial and misleading perspective on what is happening. Indeed, when one lifts the hood, so to speak, to see what is driving the media revolution, a very different picture emerges. The engine of change at this point is highly concentrated corporate power, which pulls the strings to dominate our existence so as to maximize return to shareholders. A secondary, yet no less significant purpose, is to protect the corporation's role—and corporate power in general—from being subjected to the public scrutiny and political debate it so richly deserves. This combination is a poison pill for democracy.

Yet in our American democracy the issue of media reform barely registers. The structures of our media, the concentration of its ownership, the role that it plays in shaping the lives of our children, in commercializing our culture, and in warping our elections, has been off-limits. When we examine the reality of media in the year 2002, however, it becomes clear that this circumstance must shift.

Dominated by ten corporations

The argument for making media an issue can be found, above all, by surveying the contemporary media landscape.

In 2002, the U.S. media system is dominated by about ten transnational conglomerates including Disney, AOL Time Warner, News Corporation, Viacom, Vivendi Universal, Sony, Liberty, Bertelsmann, AT&T-Comcast, and General Electric (NBC). Their media revenues range from roughly $8 billion to $35 billion per year. These firms tend to have holdings in numerous media sectors. AOL Time Warner, for example, ranks among the largest players in film production, recorded music, TV show production, cable TV channels, cable TV systems, book publishing, magazine publishing, and Internet service provision. This first tier owns all the commercial television networks, all the major Hollywood studios, four of the five firms that sell 90 percent of the music in the United States, a majority of the cable TV systems, all or part of most of the successful cable TV channels, and much, much, more. The great profit in media today comes from taking a movie or TV show and milking it for maximum return through spin-off books, CDs, video games, and merchandise. Hence it is virtually impossible to compete as a "stand-alone" movie studio, TV network, or music company, when one's competitors are part of vast empires. This has fueled the massive conglomeration rush of the past fifteen years.

Another twelve to fifteen firms, which do from $2 or $3 billion to $8 billion per year in business, round out the system. These firms—like Hearst, the New York Times Company, the Washington Post Company, Cox, Advance, Tribune Company, Gannett—tend to be less developed conglomerates, focusing on only two or three media sectors.

All in all, these two dozen or so firms control the overwhelming percentage of movies, TV shows, cable systems, cable channels, TV stations, radio stations, books, magazines, newspapers, billboards, music, and TV networks that constitute the media culture that occupies one-half of the average American's life. It is an extraordinary degree of economic and social power located in very few hands. The highly concentrated market makes a mockery of the freedom of press clause in the First Amendment, which was predicated on the ability of citizens to create their own media if they so desire. A person may have the "right" to launch a new movie studio or major daily newspaper, but, except in the rare circumstances of a handful of billionaires, it is a "right" in name only. "The history of survival of start-up newspapers in markets that already have at least one daily is not a happy one," a newspaper analyst commented in 2002. "In fact, there is no history. There has never been one survivor."

The average American spent almost twelve hours per day with some form of media.

It has not always been this way. Much of this concentration has taken place in the past few decades, as technology and market imperatives made concentration and conglomeration far more attractive and necessary. Today it is impossible for the small, independent firm to be anything but a marginal player in the industries mentioned above. Most important, the flames of media concentration were fanned by a collapsing commitment on the part of the federal government to serious antitrust prosecution, a diminution of the federal standards regarding fairness, and government "deregulation," most notably the 1996 Telecommunications Act. Congressional approval of the Telecommunications Act, after only a stilted and disengaged debate, was a historic turning point in media policy making in the United States, as it permitted a consolidation of media and communication ownership that had previously been unthinkable.

"Earth-shattering" shift

In 2002, a series of developments suggest that media concentration is becoming even more extreme. For decades, a few key FCC [Federal Communications Commission] ownership regulations limited the ability of the media giants to expand. These included rules preventing the same company from owning TV stations and cable franchises in the same market, limiting the number of TV stations a single company could own, and restricting ownership of newspapers and TV stations in the same community. The FCC, under the leadership of President George W. Bush's appointed chair, Michael Powell, is expressly committed to decreasing or eliminating these and other limits on media monopoly—including the last barriers to a single corporation gaining dominance of print, broadcast, and cable communications in a single market. The multipronged strategy

of the media giants also has a legal component. In 2002, the conglomerates won cases in the federal court system tossing key ownership regulations out as unconstitutional. Only if the FCC or Congress can make a better defense of them will the regulations be preserved.

---

*A person may have the "right" to launch a new
movie studio or major daily newspaper, but, except
in the rare circumstances of a handful of
billionaires, it is a "right" in name only.*

The result of all this deregulation, should it proceed, will be an explosion of corporate deal making that will make the last decade of unprecedented media conglomeration look like a Wednesday night bingo
game at the local old folks home. For the first time, media giants that
have controlled TV station empires—Disney, News Corp., Viacom, General Electric—would be able to merge with or acquire media empires built
on cable franchises, such as AOL Time Warner and AT&T-Comcast. As
Blair Levin, a former FCC chief of staff, puts it, the ruling "allows for a
powerful new entity we have never seen before—something that com-
bines both cable and broadcasting assets." Include the ability to merge
with the giant newspaper chains and you have a recipe for what Gene
Kimmelman of the Consumers Union calls an "earth-shattering" shift in
media ownership patterns. "The end result could be the most massive
consolidation in media this nation has ever seen," says Kimmelman. . . .

Advertisers determine content

In this light, it is worth considering the status of the long-standing conflict between "church and state" in media; this refers to the ability of journalists and creative workers to conduct their affairs without having output
determined by what serves the immediate interests of advertisers, or owners for that matter. In conventional wisdom, the U.S. media system has
been at its best when the divider between "church and state"—especially,
though not exclusively, in journalism—has been pronounced and respected. That way media users can regard the articles and news and entertainment programs they read, see, and hear in the media as reflecting the
best judgment of media workers, not the surreptitious bribe of a commercial interest. Nowhere has the collapse of editorial integrity been more pronounced than in magazine publishing. As the late Alexander Liberman,
legendary editorial director of Condé Nast, noted in 1999, advertisers
"have too much power. They determine, if not specifically, then generally
what magazines are now." A series of scandals in the late 1990s affirmed
what has been suspected: Advertisers have tremendous control over the
editorial copy in U.S. magazines, and editors who are discomfited by this
had best find employment elsewhere. "They're glitz bags," [author and social critic] Norman Mailer said of magazines in 1999. "They are so obvi-
ously driven by the ads that the ads take prominence over the stories.". . .

This said, we are not attempting to make a blanket indictment of
everything produced by the corporate media system. We are not suggest-

ing that every article or broadcast segment is foul, nor that they are all tainted, nor even that some material that is tainted cannot also be good. There are extremely talented people employed in the commercial media system, and the pressure to satisfy audiences does indeed sometimes promote excellent fare. But corporate and commercial pressures greatly undermine the overall quality of the system and skew it in ways that are not at all the result of audience demand. In the world of corporate media, the key is to attract the preferred target audience while spending as little money as possible. In the battle for consumer attention, this strongly promotes a rehashing of tried-and-true formulae, as well as the use of sex, violence, and what is termed "shock" or "gross-out" fare. In a world where people are surrounded by innumerable media options (albeit owned by numerable firms), sex and violence are proven attention getters.

Limited political coverage

Corporate control and hypercommercialism are having what may be their most devastating effects in the realm of journalism, and as journalism is the oxygen of democracy, it is here that we must devote considerable attention. . . .

The brave new world of corporate journalism manifests itself in many ways. The primary effects of tightened corporate control are a serious reduction in staff, combined with pressure to do vastly less expensive and less controversial lifestyle and feature stories. Where there is "news," it often takes the form of canned crime reports that foster unrealistic and unnecessary fears. This is the magic elixir for the bottom line. Sometimes the new world of corporate journalism is typified by blatant corporate censorship of stories that might hurt the image of the media owner. . . .

The most common and noticeable effect of the corporate noose on journalism is that it simply allows commercial values to redirect journalism to its most profitable position. As a result, relatively vast resources are deployed for news pitched at a narrow business class, and suited to their needs and prejudices; such news has come to dominate newspapers, specialty magazines, and cable television. Likewise, news for the masses increasingly consists of stories about celebrities, royal families, athletes, natural disasters, plane crashes, and train wrecks. Political coverage is limited to regurgitating what some politician says, and "good" journalism is practiced when a politician from the other side of the aisle is given a chance to respond. During the Florida recount following the 2000 election, television networks featured nightly food fights between backers of Gore and Bush, but left the real reporting on disenfranchisement of minority voters, structural flaws in the voting systems, and corrupt practices within the offices of Florida Governor Jeb Bush and Secretary of State Katherine Harris to the British Broadcasting Corporation (BBC) and other foreign broadcasters. . . .

All told, this creates a crisis for democracy. [Nineteenth-century social critic] Alexis de Tocqueville rightly celebrated the role that a free and diverse media plays not only in greasing the wheels of electoral systems but in maintaining the very structures of civil society. The nineteenth-century surveyor of the American public landscape went so far as to say of news organizations, "They maintain civilization." Who would seriously attempt to make such a statement about media in an era of round-the-clock coverage [of political scandals]?

The current caliber of journalism is decidedly unsatisfactory for a democratic society. Democratic journalism should provide a ruthless accounting of the powers-that-be and the powers-that-want-to-be, both in government and politics and in the extremely powerful corporate sector. Democratic journalism should also provide background information and a full range of viewpoints on the main social and political issues of the day. We cannot expect each news medium to provide all of these elements of a quality journalism, but in combination, a democratic media system should make this caliber of journalism readily available to the entire population. It may be true that the media are not entirely responsible for the apathy, cynicism, and depoliticization that mark U.S. electoral politics today; in fact, media executives sometimes use this lack of interest in politics to justify their declining attention to public affairs and their continuing coverage of trivial and mindless stories. However, it is also true that the lack of journalism has fanned the flames of depoliticization and contributed to U.S. electoral politics becoming a commercial contest sponsored by a small group of billionaires, in which most Americans rationally assume they have no role to play, or stake in the outcome. Presidential elections now draw, at best, no more than half of the electorate to the polls. They have become media entertainments, complete with graphics and play-by-play reports but bereft of any suggestion that citizens should—or could—actually play any more of a role in this extravaganza than they do in the Super Bowl or the Academy Awards.

> *In a world where people are surrounded by innumerable media options . . . sex and violence are proven attention getters.*

Not only is political coverage in American media increasingly empty and meaningless, there is also less and less of it. Indeed, while the amount of air time allotted the Super Bowl and the Academy Awards has increased in recent years—as prices paid for properly placed advertising skyrockets—coverage of the most fundamental workings of our democracy is getting squeezed. And without apology. Asked by the *Dallas Morning News* about slackening coverage of the 2000 presidential campaign by America's television networks, former ABC White House correspondent Sam Donaldson answered, "We are doing a very minimal amount of coverage at ABC. Outside of *Nightline* and our Sunday show, ABC News, in my opinion, has simply forfeited the field." Let's not pick on ABC, however; all the broadcast networks are cutting back, according to the watchdog group Alliance for Better Campaigns. During the 2000 presidential primary season, the Alliance reported, the networks were giving the presidential campaign 20 percent less coverage than they did in 1988—the last time the U.S. saw serious contests for the Democratic and Republican presidential nominations. Ex-CNN president Rick Kaplan told the *Philadelphia Inquirer* that the major broadcast networks had been "derelict" in their coverage of the 2000 campaign. "They're making their news divisions less important than they were. They're just getting out."

To be fair and accurate, journalism is flawed not merely due to corporate pressures to generate profits or to satisfy the political desires of the owners; the problem goes deeper than that. Much of the problem with contemporary journalism is due to the codes of professional journalism that emerged a century ago, and that remain of paramount importance in understanding journalism today. Professional journalism was a revolutionary break with the idea that the journalism of a medium—usually a newspaper at that time—would and should invariably reflect the political viewpoints of the owner. Partisan journalism, the bread and butter of Jefferson, Jackson, and Lincoln, could only be defended in an environment where there were competitive markets, and a wide range of opinion. In the highly concentrated newspaper markets that emerged by the twentieth century, partisan journalism appeared more like uncontested propaganda than anything else. In this environment, the large newspaper publishers pushed for professionalism. Their journalists would all be trained to be nonpartisan so the matter of who owned all the media and the lack of market competition were now irrelevant. As research has shown repeatedly, however, the professional code "smuggled in" the political biases of the owners, but made them now appear as nonpartisan, even objective truth.

With this in mind, let us [turn] to the three great news stories of recent times . . . each of which goes to the heart of a core democratic function of the free press. The first, the 2000 presidential election, was about whether the American people could hold a fair election for the highest office in the land. The second, the War on Terrorism, concerns how this nation arrives at the most important decision any society can make: to enter and conduct a world war with no end in sight. The third, the revelation of [failed energy company] Enron's ability to squeeze billions from taxpayers, workers, and consumers by buying off politicians right and left for its dubious deregulation schemes, speaks to the ability of journalism to hold government—and the firms it regulates—accountable for corruption.

Tough questions ignored

Let's start with the War on Terrorism. When a democracy considers whether to engage in war, the free flow of information is of dramatic significance: How can parents decide that they favor sending their sons and daughters off to fight when they lack adequate information about the causes, goals, and strategies of the proposed fight? How can citizens decide whether it is appropriate to reorder national economic priorities in order to fund an ongoing "War on Terror" when they do not even know the targets of that war? From World War I to Korea and Vietnam, presidents have lied to the American people because they believed that if the American people knew the truth, they would not support the move for war. The track record of the U.S. news media in the twentieth century is one of regularly going along with fraudulent efforts to get the nation into one war or another by the administration in power. These are considered the dark moments in the history of U.S. journalism. What is most striking in the U.S. news coverage following the September 11 attacks is how it followed this lamentable pattern. The most essential debate—the one about whether to go to war—never really occurred in Congress or the media. Tough questions were ignored. Why should we have believed that a militarized approach would be effective? Why was the United States entitled to determine—as judge, jury, and executioner—who is a terrorist or a terrorist sympathizer in this global war? What about international law?

Most conspicuous was the complete absence of comment on one of the most striking features of the war campaign—something that any credible journalist would be quick to observe were the events taking place in Russia or China or Pakistan. There are very powerful interests in the United States that greatly benefit politically and economically by the establishment of an unchecked war on terrorism. This consortium of interests can be called, to use President Eisenhower's term, the military-industrial complex. It blossomed during the Cold War when the fear of Soviet imperialism—real or alleged—justified its creation and expansion. A nation with a historically small military now had a permanent war economy, and powerful special interests—private-sector defense contractors chief among them—that benefited by its existence.

> *Not only is political coverage in American media increasingly empty and meaningless, there is also less and less of it.*

For journalists to raise issues like these did not presuppose that they opposed government policies, merely that the policies needed to be justified and explained, so the support would be substantive, not ephemeral, the result of deliberation, not manipulation. Such has not been the case. Much of mainstream U.S. journalism was bluntly propagandistic in the weeks and months following September 11. As a result, most Americans supported a war, even though they knew next to nothing about the region where U.S. soldiers would be fighting, the historical context of the battles, or the role that past military adventurism might have played in stoking the resentments that feed international anger at the United States.

Establishment bias

It is important to be clear about why the coverage has been so deplorable. It is not directly due to concentrated media ownership, or meddling CEOs, although the very firms that are now saluting "America's New War" are also going before the Bush Administration asking for ownership deregulation that will make all of them much larger and more profitable. The main reason for this distorted coverage is due to the way in which so-called "professional" journalism is practiced in the United States. To avoid the taint of partisanship, and to keep costs low, professionalism makes official or credentialed sources the basis for news stories. Reporters report what people in power say, and what they debate. This gives the news an establishment bias. Even when there is disagreement, the range of debate extends only as far as does the disagreement of those with a vested interest in limiting the scope of the discourse.

When a journalist reports what official sources are saying, or debating, she is considered "professional." When she steps outside this range of official debate to provide alternative perspectives or to raise issues those in power prefer not to discuss, she is no longer considered "professional."

In matters of international politics, "official sources" are almost interchangeable with the term "elites," as foreign policy is mostly a preserve of a wealthy and powerful few. . . . At its worst, in a case like the current war on terrorism, where the elites and official sources are unified on the core issues, the nature of our press coverage is uncomfortably close to that found in authoritarian societies with limited formal press freedom.

Many working journalists would recoil at that statement. Their response would be that professional reliance on official sources is justifiable as "democratic" because the official sources are accountable to people who are elected by the citizenry. The problem with this rationale is that it forgets a critical assumption of free press theory: Even leaders determined by election need a rigorous monitoring, the range of which cannot be determined solely by their elected opposition. Otherwise the citizenry has no way out of the status quo, no capacity to criticize or advance the political culture as a whole. If such a watchdog function grows lax, corruption invariably increases, and the electoral system decays. If journalism that goes outside the range of elite opinion is dismissed as unprofessional or partisan—and, therefore, justifiably ignored—the media merely lock in a corrupt status quo and can offer no way out. If journalists must have official sources on their side to pursue a story, it gives people in power a massive veto power over the exercise of democracy.

This problem becomes acute in a political environment like the United States, where electoral laws and campaign costs have made politics a fiefdom for the superwealthy and those who represent the superwealthy. Over ninety percent of the "hard money" contributions to congressional and presidential campaigns come from the wealthiest one percent of Americans. By relying on official sources, our journalism does not pose a democratic challenge to plutocracy, but rather cements the plutocracy in place.

"Rah-rah corporate journalists"

But the best example of the plutocracy protection principle that now defines U.S. journalism is the Enron scandal that unfolded in late 2001 and 2002. The story of Enron's collapse was shocking only because, although evidence of Enron's shady operations had been cropping up since at least the mid-1990s, the rah-rah corporate journalists of our era were falling all over themselves to praise Enron as the exemplar of the New Economy. Enron was regularly featured on *Global Finance* magazine's annual list of the "world's best global companies." Even as the collapse of Enron approached, *Fortune* magazine hailed the corporation as its "most innovative company in America."

Only when the company approached bankruptcy did it rate as anything akin to a news story—and not much of a news story at that. The corporate media had special incentive not to push the Enron story too far. Were discussion of Enron and energy policies to lead to any sustained examination of the way communication policies are produced behind closed doors in Washington—arguably the most off-limits story in U.S. journalism in our times—it would find a thick stench that would rival anything Enron has done. But that wasn't the whole of why the media missed the real story.

Although it is clear that the Enron affair is a stunning example of supreme political corruption, the coverage increasingly came to concentrate upon the business collapse of Enron, and the chicanery of [accounting firm] Arthur Andersen, rather than the sleazy methods, legal as well as illegal, in which the company used the political system to make billions of dollars ripping off consumers, taxpayers, and workers. In another era, the Enron collapse would have provoked a bigger political crisis . . . and forced dramatic action by Congress. Still, all indications are that the Enron scandal will not turn into a political crisis that will end political careers and lead to major political reform; the opposition Democrats are in no hurry to push the story to its logical political conclusion because so many of them would be implicated as well. Thus, there is no debate among official sources about the proper response to the political corruption issues raised by the Enron case. Without those official sources, "professional" journalism is restricted to a discussion that begins and ends within the limits of what those in power pursue, and the balance of the population has no one representing *its* interests. What about those who simply want the whole truth to come out? What about those who want the system changed so this sort of corruption is less likely to occur in the future? They are out of luck. This is disastrous for liberal democracy, as it suggests to citizens that even dramatic revelations of corporate and political corruption will not lead to change. If the press system cannot produce coverage that leads to peaceful and credible reform of corruption, it only means the problems will get worse and the costs of an eventual resolution significantly greater.

The media anointed Bush president

Finally, consider the manner in which the press reported President Bush's "victory" in the 2000 election. It is now clear that the majority of people in Florida who went to vote for president in November 2000 intended to vote for Al Gore. Indeed, buried in the footnotes of a recount conducted by the major news media in 2001 was the revelation that using any method that sought to quantify the actual sentiments of the actual voters the result was the same: Al Gore won Florida. And winning Florida was supposed to cinch the presidency. But Al Gore isn't president. Why is that? Or, to put it another way, why didn't the press coverage assure that the true winner would assume office? After all, if the free press cannot guarantee the integrity of elections, what good is it? The primary reason is due to sourcing: Throughout November and early December of 2000, the news media were being told by all Republicans that the Republicans had won the election and Al Gore was trying to steal it. The Democrats, on the other hand, were far less antagonistic and showed much less enthusiasm to fight for what they had won. Hence, the news coverage, reflecting what their sources were telling them, tended to reflect the idea that the Republicans had won and the Democrats were grasping for straws. When [journalist] Greg Palast broke the story in Britain in November 2000 that the Florida Republicans had systematically and illegally excluded thousands of poor Floridians from voting—in itself, certainly enough to cost Gore the state—no U.S. mainstream news medium dared pick it up, even though the story was painstakingly well documented. Why? Most likely because journalists would have been out on their own, since the Democrats had elected not to fight on this issue. Once the Supreme Court made its final decision, the media announced that our national nightmare was over—neglecting to note that, according to most polls, Americans would have been perfectly willing to have the process go on in order to identify a clear winner. The media had helped anoint a president. The only losers were the irrelevant and powerless souls who clung to the belief that whoever gets the most votes should win the election, and that the press should tell the whole truth and let the chips fall where they may.

"Professional" journalism is restricted to a discussion that begins and ends within the limits of what those in power pursue, and the balance of the population has no one representing its interests.

Having played the role that it did in picking the president, the media was in no position to criticize the Bush Administration. This explains at least some of the willingness of the mainstream U.S. news media to suspend criticism of President Bush almost *in toto* [totally] after September 11. Having foisted the moronic child of privilege upon the American people, it became necessary in a moment of national anguish to remake him as another Lincoln, albeit one who preferred lifting weights to reading books.

When the recount report containing data that seemed to confirm that Gore had won Florida was released two months after September 11, what was striking was how almost all the press reported that the results were mixed or that Bush had won. Major newspapers and television networks reached this "conclusion" only through the Olympic-style gymnastic twist of analyzing the data from the standpoint of what the Gore campaign had requested in November of the year before. The identity of the actual winner of the actual election in Florida—i.e., the person who most of the voters preferred—seemed not to interest the press one whit. In a manner of thinking, the press had no choice but to provide this interpretation. If the media conceded that Gore, in fact, had won the race in Florida, it would have made people logically ask, "why didn't the media determine this when it mattered?" Moreover, a concession that the United States had an unelected president would make the laudatory coverage of President Bush after September 11 look increasingly like the sort of paeans to "maximum leaders" expected from the news media in tinhorn dictatorships. As soon as the leaders are not the product of free and fair elections, they lose credibility; with that development, the "professional" reliance on official sources, which is wobbly by democratic standards to begin with, collapses. . . .

[A] defense of the existing order is that this is the "natural" American system; if someone is dissatisfied with it, that person should shut up or move to another country, preferably on the other side of the world. The "love-it-or-leave-it" theory, aggressively advanced by the likes of millionaire radio personality Rush Limbaugh, holds that the First Amendment has authorized two dozen profit-seeking transnational corporations to rule U.S. media with ample government subsidies but with no public "interference" otherwise. This is an argument that does not stand up to any historical scrutiny. It is true that the First Amendment prohibits congressional interference with a free press; however, it does not therefore authorize concentrated corporate and advertiser domination of the press. Imagine a parallel phenomenon in the practice of religion: If a handful of faiths were using their accumulated resources and their lobbying influence with government to gain dominance in the spiritual life of the land while forcing faiths with different ideas and values out of the public sphere, would First Amendment absolutists argue that this was the intent of the "freedom of religion" protection? If they tried to do so, they would be stymied by the courts, laughed out of any serious debate, and appropriately labeled as self-serving theocratic totalitarians.

The First Amendment belongs to all Americans, not just the billionaire investors in a handful of giant media firms, and it is based on the notion that democracy demands a press that serves us all. We are not arguing for government censorship of the commercial media—in fact, we oppose efforts in that direction—but we think efforts to reduce the power of Wall Street and Madison Avenue, and to increase the role of Main Street and every other sector of the population, in the running of our media system are entirely consistent with the meaning of the First Amendment.

6

Conservative Talk Show Hosts Poison Political Discourse

Eric Alterman

Eric Alterman is an award-winning author who has written several best-selling books. His work has also appeared in many national magazines including the Nation, Rolling Stone, Mother Jones, Elle, *and* World Policy Journal.

More than one in five American adults say they listen to talk radio at least once a week. And even conservatives agree that this powerful medium is dominated by commentators who espouse a right-wing viewpoint. Rush Limbaugh is the most popular commentator on talk radio even though many of his diatribes against Democrats are less than accurate while some consist of outright lies. Despite his questionable commentary, Limbaugh has galvanized his listeners to support Republican politicians and is credited with helping Republicans gain unprecedented political power in recent years. Limbaugh has spawned dozens of right-wing imitators including Matt Drudge whose unverifiable articles on the Drudge Report Web site have been credited with helping bring about the impeachment of President Bill Clinton in 1998. Drudge now has his own radio talk show and has filled in for Rush Limbaugh when the latter was in treatment for drug addiction. Both Drudge and Limbaugh regale media consumers with rumor, innuendo, and vicious personal attacks on Democrats and liberals. This extremism has popularized attack politics and has led to the poisoning of all political discourse in the United States.

Talk radio is a great deal more popular—and powerful—than most of us realize. Twenty-two percent of all Americans surveyed say they listen. In some major cities, the number is as high as 40 percent. Conservative domination of the talk-radio airwaves is so extensive as to be undisputed, even by the usual suspects. There's not a single well-known liberal talk-show host in the nation and barely a host who does not at least lean well in the direction of the extreme right. The most popular shows are hosted by Rush Limbaugh, G. Gordon Liddy, Oliver North, Sean Hannity, Armstrong Williams, Blanquita Collum, Michael Savage, Neil Boortz, Bob Grant, Bob Dornan, Michael Medved, Michael Reagan, Dr. Laura Schlesinger, Howard Stern, Don Imus, Michael Graham, Ken Hamblin, and Laura Ingraham. Every single one is a movement conservative with politics located at the extreme far-right end of the political spectrum. So far to the right is the general pack of talk-show hosts that, early in the Clinton Administration, G. Gordon Liddy felt empowered to instruct listeners on the best way to assassinate U.S. government officials from the Bureau of Alcohol, Tobacco, and Firearms without receiving much in the way of censure from this community. (His exact words were "Head shots. Head shots.") Once, during a joint C-Span appearance with a right-wing talk-show host and activist, Paul Weyrich, I challenged him to condemn Liddy's statement and he refused, as he put it, to "criticize a brother talk-show host," even for advocating the murder of U.S. government officials. When Bill O'Reilly joined the ranks of radio talk-show hosts in the spring of 2002, he could legitimately claim to be a relative liberal in their midst. Even the Internet gossip Matt Drudge, no stranger to irresponsible right-wing rumor-mongering, says that when he has a story that is "playing among the wing nuts, this tells me it's going to be a huge talk-radio thing."

Indeed, because the radio business has become so centralized in recent years, it is easy for talk-show hosts to spread themselves across the dial with incredible speed. O'Reilly's show debuted in the spring of 2002 with 205 stations, ahead of Michael Medved's 130, Sean Hannity's 150 or so, and Laura Ingraham's nearly 200 markets. But O'Reilly was still way behind Limbaugh's market share, which has gone as high as 650 stations and anywhere from fifteen to twenty million listeners, depending on whose statistics you prefer. Few progressives are ever given shows, and efforts such as Gary Hart's and Mario Cuomo's haven't amounted to much. The left-wing Texas populist Jim Hightower appeared to be building a strong regional audience back in the mid-1990s, but he was highly critical of Disney and its owner, Michael Eisner. Not long after Disney bought the station, Hightower's show was abruptly canceled. KGO in San Francisco, perhaps alone in the country, boasts two liberal hosts, Bernie Ward and Ray Taliafero, whose shows appear at 10 P.M. to 1 A.M. and 1 A.M. to 5 A.M.—not exactly primetime. . . .

Elimination of the Fairness Doctrine

Edward Monks, a Eugene, Oregon, attorney, calculates that in his city, conservatives enjoy a 4,000-to-zero hour advantage over liberals on the radio. He wrote in *The Register-Guard:* "Political opinions expressed on talk radio are approaching the level of uniformity that would normally be achieved only in a totalitarian society. . . . There is nothing fair, balanced or democratic about it." Monk noted that as recently as 1974, such domination would have been not only inconceivable, but illegal. Back then, the Federal Communications Commission [FCC] was still demanding "strict adherence to the [1949] Fairness Doctrine as the single most important requirement of operation in the public interest—the sine qua non [indis-

pensable condition] for grant for renewal of license." This view was rati-
fied by the U.S. Supreme Court in 1969 when it reaffirmed the people's
right to a free exchange of opposing views, with roughly equal time given
to all sides, if demanded, on the public airwaves. The doctrine was over-
turned by the Reagan-appointed FCC in 1987. The chairman then, Mark
Fowler, made clear his view that "the perception of broadcasters as community trustees should be replaced by a view of broadcasters as marketplace participants." Meanwhile, media companies, together with cigarette
and beer companies, working with Republican Senator Bob Packwood, set
up the Freedom of Expression Foundation to fight the fairness doctrine in
the U.S. Court of Appeals for Washington, D.C. The companies won in a
2-to-1 decision. . . . President Reagan vetoed attempts by Congress to re-
instate the doctrine, and the net result has been the complete far-right
domination of the nation's airwaves, owing entirely to what analysts call
"marketplace realities."

---

*"Political opinions expressed on talk radio are
approaching the level of uniformity that would
normally be achieved only in a totalitarian society.
. . . There is nothing fair, balanced or democratic
about it."*

The amazing career of Rush Limbaugh owes a great deal to that moment in history. It is testament to just how well success succeeds in the U.S.
media, regardless of accuracy, fairness, or even common sense. Limbaugh's
legendary lies and mythological meanderings have been rewarded not only
with legions of listeners, but also with incredible riches—a contract said to
be worth $250 million over seven years. It has also won him the respect of
the media establishment. Limbaugh, for instance, has been treated to
laudatory coverage in *Time* and *Newsweek* and was invited by host Tim
Russert of *Meet the Press* to be a guest commentator on what is certainly the
most influential political program on television. And yet Limbaugh is, to
put it bluntly, deranged. Fairness and Accuracy in Reporting has published
an entire book of Rushisms that have turned out to be false, unsubstantiated, or just plain wacko. It is not just, as Maureen Dowd put it, his obses-
sion with "feminazis," "environmental wackos," Anita Hill, Jesse Jackson,
Hillary Clinton, Teddy Kennedy, Mario Cuomo, homeless advocates, dol-
phins, spotted owls, trees, "commie libs," and "the arts and croissant
crowd." Limbaugh pushes the bounds of good taste in any medium, not to
mention simple human decency, such as the time on his now-defunct TV
show, he asked, "Did you know there's a White House dog?" and held up
a photo of then-thirteen-year-old Chelsea Clinton. Another time, he
showed a picture of Secretary of Labor Robert Reich that showed him from
the forehead up, as though that were all of his frame that the camera could
capture. (The diminutive Reich had a bone disease as a child.) Even when
Limbaugh is not insulting the looks of young girls or making fun of childhood diseases, his ideological flights of fancy should leave any even re-
motely discerning listeners shaking their heads in disbelief.

Still, Limbaugh can have a real impact on issues, irrespective of the crackpot notions that inform his views. When, in June 2002, the Bush Administration gave up its . . . battle to deny the reality of global warming—a fact of life accepted by the entire panoply of world governments as well as virtually every climatologist of note in all of these nations, Rush was aghast. He knew better.

> When I first became aware of this story Sunday night, I thought about what I would say on Monday's program: "Well, folks, guess what? I have been wrong about global warming. The president says it is happening and that human beings are causing it, so I've been wrong." I couldn't say that because I don't think I am wrong. There are too many scientists out there whom I implicitly trust who have proven to me these predictions are basically apocalyptic doom and gloom based on raw emotion. Even the global warming advocates, to this day, will not tell you it is definitively happening.

Recall that the Bush Administration was not actually proposing to do anything about global warming. It had, in fact, put itself in the absurd position of predicting horrific consequences of global warming and yet remaining politically unwilling or unable to avert them. One might therefore draw the conclusion that Bush's cabinet reluctantly came to their long-averted conclusion. . . . But Rush was not fooled. Bush and company had, for reasons he did not explain, caved into "the environmentalist wacko coalition." The president had morphed into "George W. Algore." (Within twenty-four hours the White House retreated, retracting the president's admission that global warming was, in fact, real. In related news, the White House also announced that gravity was just a theory, too.). . .

Even more bizarre than these fusillades is the following transcript, taken from Limbaugh's program on July 20, 2001, in which he actually seemed to make a serious argument that Tom Daschle, leader of the Democratic majority in the Senate, was none other than the Fallen One, the Duke of Darkness, Satan himself. I quote from an extended transcript as published on the Web site, Spinsanity.com:

> I have a question for you, folks, and I know that this is going . . . you have to listen very carefully here, this is going to push the envelope. . . . How many different versions of Satan, the devil, have you seen in your life? I mean, the comic book devil with the red face and the horns, seen that one. We've seen the Satanic devil of the horror films. We've seen the devil portrayed as just an average man, a human being, in the movie *Rosemary's Baby*. We've seen the comic devil of TV shows. We've even seen the smooth, tempting devil in Hollywood movies. Is Tom Daschle simply another way to portray a devil?
>
> . . . There is no desire on Daschle's part to bring people together. There certainly is no bipartisanship flowing through his veins, nor is he leading any bipartisan effort. There is no working with the president of any of this. He's criticizing Bush, he's attempting to further the notion that Bush is ille-

gitimate, incompetent, unintelligent. . . . Just yesterday, as Bush winged his way to Europe on a crucial mission to lead our allies into the twenty-first century, with Europe's flagging economy, talking about mutual defense in the twenty-first century, realistic environmental solutions, solutions for world poverty, . . . and not allowing the United States to be robbed blind by the U.N. and the poor nations of the world, up pops "El Diablo," Tom Daschle, and his devilish deviltry, claiming that George Bush is incompetent, criticizing Bush at the very moment he is engaging in these efforts to improve our relationship with these world leaders. . . . Hang in there, folks. Now don't go bonkers—the devil comes in many disguises as we all know. . . . Let me stretch this analogy just a little bit farther. What would your reaction be if I were to say that I think Daschle has cast a spell on the media?

Honored by Republicans

Listening to Limbaugh, the idea that he enjoys genuine power in the political life of the nation leaves you shaking your head in awe and amazement. But it is impossible to ignore. Limbaugh's radio audience is the largest any program on the medium has enjoyed since the advent of television. President George H.W. Bush invited him for a White House sleepover, as well as to be his honored guest at his State of the Union address, seated next to Barbara Bush, in a demonstration of fealty and respect. Shortly thereafter, in 1993, *National Review* termed him "the leader of the opposition." William Bennett averred that Limbaugh "may be the most consequential person in political life at the moment." When the Republicans took the House back in 1994 in a profound and humiliating rebuke to President Clinton, Limbaugh's broadcast received a lion's share of the credit. *Washington Post* media reporter Howard Kurtz even defended nonsense like the above as "policy oriented." As Newt Gingrich's former press secretary Tony Blankley noted,

> After Newt, Rush was the single most important person in securing a Republican majority in the House of Representatives after 40 years of Democratic Party rule. Rush's powerful voice was the indispensable factor, not only in winning in 1994, but in holding the House for the next three election cycles. At a time when almost the entire establishment media ignored or distorted our message of renewal, Rush carried (and often improved) the message to the heartland. And where Rush led, the other voices of talk radio followed.

This influence cannot be said to have diminished markedly during the past decade, even after Limbaugh lost his most-favored targets when the Clintons left the White House. Much to his chagrin as a [John] McCain supporter, [political analyst] William Kristol credits Limbaugh with rallying conservatives behind Bush during the 2000 presidential primaries. "He helped make it the orthodox conservative position that McCain was utterly unacceptable and also that Bush was fine, neither of which were intuitively obvious if you're a conservative," Kristol said. Mc-

Cain's South Carolina political adviser, Richard M. Quinn, concurred, adding that the Arizona senator never recovered, in his opinion, from Limbaugh's repeated descriptions of the conservative Republican as a "liberal" in an extremely conservative state. "I never polled on the impact of Limbaugh," Quinn told the *New York Times*. "But anecdotally, I heard it all the time. You would hear on the street repetition of what Rush was saying about McCain. There was a general sense in the campaign that Limbaugh was definitely hurting us." Blankley put it bluntly: "Given the closeness of the election, but for Rush Limbaugh's broadcasts, we would now be led by President Al Gore." In the 2002 midterm elections, NBC used him as one of its analysts. And on September 11, 2002, Vice President Cheney had just one planned interview on his schedule to mark the hallowed anniversary of the tragedy of a year before: a phone interview with Rush Limbaugh. Cheney canceled his appearance at the last minute, citing his removal from public view to a "secure location," under the raised state of alert declared by federal officials as the reason for his no-show. Apparently his "secure location" did not contain a telephone.

Influence of the Internet

It is particularly impressive that Limbaugh has managed to maintain his popularity following the loss of his biggest target, Bill Clinton, and the eclipse of radio beginning in the mid-1990's explosion of the Internet. The explosion of the use of the Web may prove to be one of the great technological transformations in the history of human communications. By the end of 2001, a single site, www.yahoo.com, boasted more than 70 million users, with an annual increase rate of 18 percent. While the Internet has enormous value for more reasons and purposes than can be profitably counted, for scholars, for communities, for journalists, and for just goofing off, for political purposes it turns out to have a great deal in common with radio. Not unlike the way in which the irresponsible right-wing talk-show network forms its own self-referential information circuit, "news" on the Net is passed along from one site to another with little concern for its credibility. Also like radio, this tactic of combining the unverifiable with a metaphorical microphone has been perfected by the far right to create a doubly deceitful dynamic of ideological extremism, false information, and accusation against which truth—and liberalism—have little chance to compete. Rush Limbaugh, meet Matt Drudge.

> *"Rush was the single most important person in securing a Republican majority in the House of Representatives after 40 years of Democratic Party rule."*

While the Net is economically dominated by a tiny number of large corporations, just like television and radio, the information that appears on it is not. Standards for established news services with a net presence have by and large been maintained; however, the true story of political news on the Net is with the small, right-wing sites that use the Web almost as effectively as they use talk radio. Web sites like the Drudge Report, NewsMax.com, WorldNetDaily.com, FreeRepublic.com, Townhall.com, Lucianne.com, JewishWorldReview.com, and National Review Online boast regular readers in the millions. What's more, they are dedicated readers and in many cases, like the Limbaugh audience, so far to the right as to tend toward outer space. For instance, Joseph Farah, a columnist for Worldnet, warned his readers in October 2002, "The Democrats—far too many of them—are evil, pure and simple. They have no redeeming social value. They are outright traitors themselves or apologists for treasonous behavior. They are enemies of the American people and the American way of life." On Lucianne.com, a number of posters celebrated the plane crash that killed [Senator] Paul Wellstone, his wife, and daughter, in late October 2002 and expressed the hope that [Senator] Ted Kennedy would meet a similar fate. Even further out in the right wing ozonosphere, is the site FreeRepublic.com. While posts terming Gore a "traitor" are commonplace, alongside the addresses and phone numbers of allegedly liberal politicians and judges, a UPI story unearthed one user who sympathized with [convicted Oklahoma City bomber] Timothy McVeigh and another who called him a "modern-day Paul Revere." According to figures published in the *New York Times*, the average "Freeper" Web visit lasts an amazing five hours and fourteen minutes. It's not a hobby for these people, it's a life. . . .

Unsubstantiated rumor

Undoubtedly the biggest star of Net journalism—its Rush Limbaugh if you will—is . . . Matt Drudge, who claims more than 100 million visits a month to his bare-bones, next-to-no-graphics site. Like Limbaugh, Drudge professes nothing but contempt for the mainstream news establishment. Viewed, he crows, "daily not only by presidents and world leaders, CEOs, anchormen and top media editors," Drudge claims to be "powered" only by endless curiosity and a love of freedom. Of course with numbers like his, the media he disdains cannot help but celebrate him. Drudge was named one of *Newsweek*'s new media stars and *People*'s Twenty-Five Most Intriguing People. The *American Journalism Review* ran a cover story entitled, "Journalism in the Era of Drudge and [*Hustler* publisher Larry] Flynt," and the *Columbia Journalism Review* cited his outing of the Monica Lewinsky affair in 1998 as one of the ten key dates in the media history of the twentieth century.

Originally an amateur Hollywood gossip who picked through garbage cans to get his goods, Drudge became an overnight phenomenon as a kind of bulletin board for unsubstantiated political rumor and right-wing character attacks. Drudge describes his work habit as sitting in his apartment "petting the cat and watching the wires—that's all I do." But he also receives a great deal of e-mail. One of his favorite tactics is to steal a working journalist's story—leaked to him internally—and post its still-in-the-works details on his Web site before the author can publish them. His big moment in media history consisted of little more than posting the purloined work of *Newsweek*'s Michael Isikoff, while the magazine's editors sought further confirmation before publishing it. Drudge did it again when NBC News was trying to decide how to handle an unsubstantiated twenty-one-year-old accusation of sexual assault against President Clinton. Drudge rarely bothers to independently verify his stories, so he often appears prescient—when, in fact, he is simply overlooking what is widely understood to be the essence of journalism. Tim Russert learned this to his chagrin when Drudge posted three stories on his site about the Buffalo-born newsman's considering a run for governor of New York. "All three stories—they are just plain dead wrong," Russert complained. "And he never called me about them, never." The only surprising thing here is Russert's surprise.

Drudge became an overnight phenomenon as a kind of bulletin board for unsubstantiated political rumor and right-wing character attacks.

Drudge is a self-described misfit with few social graces, and modesty is certainly not one of them. Drudge calls his apartment "the most dangerous newsroom in America." "If I'm not interesting, the world's not interesting," he writes. "And if I'm boring, you're boring." Despite his disdain for traditional news ethics, and a lack of any discernible effort in the areas of reporting or punditry, Drudge's impact is huge. He counts his hits in the millions and can single-handedly drive hundreds of thousands—sometimes millions—of readers to any story he posts on the Web. When he purloined and posted Isikoff's Lewinsky scoop, he jump-started a political meltdown that led to the only impeachment of an elected president in American history. When he then went on to post the story of Clinton's alleged mulatto "love child," he made a national fool of himself, but hurt no one, save those gullible and irresponsible media outlets—most notably [media magnate] Rupert Murdoch's *New York Post* and [leader of the Moonies cult] Sun Myung Moon's *Washington Times*—who trusted him and reprinted it. But when he posted a malicious lie about Clinton adviser and ex-journalist Sidney Blumenthal having "a spousal abuse past that has been effectively covered up," replete with "court records of Blumenthal's violence against his wife," Drudge attacked an innocent man. But even this did not seem to hurt Drudge's reputation. Much of the media preferred Drudge to Blumenthal, whom many reporters resented for personal and professional reasons. In none of these cases did Drudge profess regret, though he did retract his false accusation against Blumenthal before the latter launched a libel suit against him. As for the Clinton "love child" concoction, Drudge bragged, "I'd do it again."

Character assassination

During the Lewinsky crisis, Drudge became so big the Internet could no longer contain him. He was given his own television program on Fox, where he was free to spout unconfirmed rumors with fellow conservative conspiracy nuts until he was informed by management that he would not be allowed to show a *National Enquirer* photo of a tiny hand emerging from the womb during a spina bifida operation on the fetus. Drudge wanted to use the photo as part of his campaign against legal abortion. When even the Fox executives found this idea not only repulsive but misleading, Drudge quit the show. Roger Ailes, whose brilliant idea it had been to hire Drudge after watching him spout baseless conspiracy theories on Russert's program, complained, "He wants to apply Internet standards, which are nonexistent, to journalism, and journalism has real standards. It can't work that way." It should come as no surprise to anyone that Drudge is also a successful force in radio, with a two-hour Sunday evening show hosted by ABC that is heard in all fifty states and literally hundreds of major markets.

Drudge also published a book—well, sort of a book. The tone was "written" with the assistance of the late Julia Phillips. Of the 247 pages contained in *The Drudge Manifesto*, the reader is treated to forty blank pages; thirty-one pages filled with fan mail; twenty-four pages of old Drudge Reports; a thirteen-page Q & A from Drudge's National Press Club speech; ten pages of titles and the like; six pages of quotes from various personalities like Ms. Lewinsky and Madonna; four pages of a chat transcript; and, well, a great deal more filler. That leaves the reader with just 112 pages or barely 45 percent of actual book. (And even nine of these are Drudge poetry.)

[Drudge] jump-started a political meltdown that led to the only impeachment of an elected president in American history.

But even with all the strikes any journalist could imagine and then some against him, Drudge still gets results for his combination of nasty innuendo and right-wing politics, often by planting items that would be picked up by allegedly respectable journalists in national newspapers. In the Arkansas Senate race of 2002, the Associated Press reported that Democrat Mark Pryor found himself forced to respond "to an item on the Drudge Report Web site of Internet gossip Matt Drudge" in a lightly sourced story that alleged the hiring of an illegal immigrant for housekeeping duties. (In fact the woman in question later signed a sworn affidavit testifying to the fact that she was a legal U.S. resident and had been paid to lie.) In May of the same year, for example, Drudge carried a report that ex-conservative journalist David Brock, whose *Blinded by the Right* embarrassed virtually the entire movement, had suffered a "breakdown" while writing the book and had to be hospitalized—something Brock reluctantly confirmed when contacted. Drudge did not mention on his site that he had considerable reason to hold a grudge against Brock, who had published in his book that he received an e-mail from the Internet snoop that said he wished the two could be "fuck buddies." (Brock is an open homosexual. Drudge is not.) As the gay journalist Michelangelo Signorile wrote, "You'd think that no respectable journalist would further the new Drudge sludge on Brock, at least not without a fuller explanation that included Drudge's possible motives." But in fact the *Washington Post* did publish it—or at least the parts Drudge wanted published, leaving out any discussion of his motives—and adding quotes from three conservatives who continued the character assassination of Brock that Drudge initiated. Nowhere in the *Post* item did the newspaper attempt to establish any journalistic relevance to the item. . . .

The echo-chamber effect

Just before Election Day 2002, Drudge and Limbaugh combined, together with Brit Hume of Fox News and the *Wall Street Journal* editorial page, to effect a smear against the Democratic Socialists of America (DSA) and, by extension, the late Senator Wellstone's re-election campaign. This episode too had all the trademarks of the conservative echo-chamber effect, including unproven innuendo, inaccuracy, repeated cavalier use of unchecked facts, all in the service of a clear political/ideological goal. As reported by Brian Keefer of Spinsanity, DSA posted a pop-up advertisement on its site on October 9 seeking contributions to pay the cost of bringing young people to Minnesota, where same-day registration is legal, to help register Wellstone voters in what was certain to be a close race. Shortly after the advertisement appeared, however, a local conservative organization sent out a press release in which it manipulated the original text to make it appear that DSA was planning to transport people not to register Minnesotans to vote, but to vote themselves, with the hopes of stealing the election.

Drudge saw the story in a local paper and headlined his site's line: "Socialists Sending People to MN to Illegally Vote for Wellstone." This apparently sent Limbaugh into action, as the radio host melodramatically informed his listeners, "DSA has been caught." With his typical respect for accuracy, Rush added, "You can go in there and register and vote and split the same day, you can go home, you don't even have to spend the night in Minnesota and freeze if you don't want to, you can go in there and vote and leave." Next up was Fox News's Brit Hume, who announced to that network's viewers, "The Democratic Socialists of America, which bill themselves as the largest socialist organization in the country, is raising tax-deductible money to send you people to the state of Minnesota, where they can take advantage of same-day registration to vote for the liberal incumbent Paul Wellstone." These reports apparently inspired the *Journal* editors who—again, contrary to all available evidence—insisted, "The Democratic Socialists of America recently posted an ad on their Web site inviting tax-deductible contributions to 'bring young people to Minnesota' to vote in the close U.S. Senate race there." As Keefer noted, while the loosely worded ad did originally raise questions about whether tax-deductible funds were being properly used for issue advocacy—and hence was rewritten for clarifying purposes—never in any of its texts did it even imply, much less encourage, anyone but Minnesotans to pick their own senator. It is perfectly legal in that state to encourage people to vote and even to take them to the polls.

Of course, Wellstone's death made the effects of this story moot, but cases like the above demonstrate just how profoundly journalistic times are a-changing. And the result of these changes is yet another victory for conservatives and scandal-mongers—and in Drudge and Limbaugh's cases, both at once—who seek to poison our political discourse with a combination of character assassination, ideological invective, and unverified misinformation. The resulting loss of credibility for phantom SCLM [So-Called Liberal Media] bespeaks not only the profession's misfortune, but democracy's as well.

7

Conservative Talk Radio Serves a Useful Purpose

John LeBoutillier

John LeBoutillier is a NewsMax.com pundit, a former U.S. congressman from New York, and a political commentator on many national talk show programs, including the Today *show, ABC's* 20/20, Nightline, *and CNN's* Crossfire.

Some liberals believe that right-wing talk radio shows have persuaded former Democrats to embrace conservative beliefs. In fact, most people who listen to talk radio are already conservative. They are fed up with the liberal bias they see in the mainstream media and are grateful for a forum for their views. While a few wealthy liberals are planning to start a left-wing talk radio network, they will find that it is not wanted or needed. Their liberal messages will fall on deaf ears in a radio format patronized mainly by conservatives.

Yesterday [February 17, 2003] in the *New York Times* it was announced that a rich group of liberals—led by Sheldon and Anita Drobny of Chicago, longtime backers of the Clintons and Al Gore—are donating $10 million to finance a "liberal talk show network" around the country.

Their purpose?

To counter what they see as the conservative slant of talk radio hosts around the nation and thus to alter the "political" trend *to the right* in this country.

Guess what?

This will be a total flop.

Because these lefties just *don't get it.*

For liberals there *already is a liberal talk radio network.* It is called National Public Radio.

For other talk radio listeners, the *very last thing they want to hear is liberal ideas.* And this is what liberals like Bill Clinton, who recently complained about the influence of [right-wing commentators] Rush Limbaugh, Sean Hannity and Bill O'Reilly, and the Drobnys, do not understand: The great majority of talk radio listeners are sick and tired of the basic liberal message of more government to solve our problems.

In fact, talk radio listeners are *more discerning* than average people. They are also better read, more knowledgeable and more interested in current events.

Listeners already conservative

Liberals like the Clintons and the Drobnys have disdain for average people and believe Rush and Sean are "brainwashing" their listeners into toeing the GOP line. Nothing could be further from the truth; these listeners are already conservative—and are ecstatic in a pop culture crammed with anti-Americanism to find someone with whom they agree.

No wonder the Clinton News Network (CNN) on TV has fallen in the ratings to Fox, which appeals to the *very same audience as do most talk radio shows*. CNN's on-air bias and culture are out of synch with cable news viewers the very same way liberal talk radio hosts don't "fit" the basic talk radio audience.

For liberals there already is a liberal talk radio network. *It is called National Public Radio.*

The Drobnys and the Clintons think the problem is the "medium"—when in fact their problem is their message. Big Government, a culture of lies and an amoral personal approach to life encompass today's liberal point of view. And that simply won't sell to the millions of patriotic Americans who use talk radio as a way to commune with like-minded citizens in a new form of national town hall.

Liberals—who have caused most of the problems we have in this country—now call themselves "progressives" because most people cringe at the thought of listening to more "liberals" and more "liberalism." It is typical liberal/leftist thought to try to jam a talk radio network down the radio industry's throat from the top down just the way they have jammed social and economic policy from Washington down the throats of average Americans.

America—thank goodness—does not work that way. In radio, if a host can't get good ratings, he/she is getting canned—period! Al Franken, an entertaining comedian, is going to have to earn an audience—not be given one by fiat.

So many liberals have tried—and all have failed. True, there are pockets of liberalism like New York City and Berkeley where a leftist can survive on the air. But to make such a host a national figure just is not going to happen.

What the Drobnys and Clintons need to do is simple: Forget trying to hijack talk radio as a medium to infect with their failed message. Instead, they need to change their message first—and then see if there is an audience for it.

8

Case Study of Conservative Bias: The *American Spectator*'s Crusade Against Bill Clinton

Charles Donefer

Charles Donefer is a reporter and the managing editor for the Johns Hopkins News-Letter.

Bill Clinton was one of the most investigated presidents in American history. Throughout his eight years in the White House, the president was accused of crimes ranging from cocaine smuggling to murder. While the president did lie to a grand jury when denying his affair with White House intern Monica Lewinsky, none of the other charges against Clinton were ever proved. After Clinton left office, it was revealed that conservative billionaire Richard Mellon Scaife had used his personal wealth—and a newspaper and magazine he owned—to spread rumors, innuendo, and lies about Clinton in the press. These scurrilous news stories drove countless right-wing radio talk shows and were reported in the mainstream press. In turn, the media stories were used by Clinton's political enemies in Congress to justify a half-dozen costly investigations that never resulted in any charges against the president. The smear campaign that Scaife termed the "Arkansas Project," named after Clinton's home state, shows how a single owner of a newspaper and magazine can nearly topple a president.

I magine suddenly realizing that a shadowy cabal with nearly unlimited funding and a legion of people who think you are pure evil is out to get you. Then imagine being laughed at as you desperately seek help from those you think might listen. You may think that this is just another horror movie plot—and it is—but it has a political parallel.

Everybody laughed at then–first lady Hillary Clinton when she went on the Today Show in 1998 to claim that her husband was the victim of a "vast right-wing conspiracy." At the time, Bill Clinton was under heavy partisan fire for the Monica Lewinsky situation. Hillary's assertion that there was a conspiracy attacking her and her husband was laughed at. Rush Limbaugh, [Speaker of the House] Newt Gingrich, *Washington Times* columnists and others were alternately amused at accusations of right-wing collusion and proud to be thought of as part of it.

Money was used mainly to pay journalists who have admitted to lying.

Despite all of the mockery she received for making the statement, Hillary was right. We now know without a doubt that there was a coordinated, secretive and well-financed organization that attempted to dig up dirt on President Clinton or lie about it when none could be found. Ominously enough, it was called the Arkansas Project, and this is its story.

Paying journalists to lie

In the early 1990s, publishing magnate and right-wing philanthropist Richard Mellon Scaife donated funds, which would end up totaling over two million dollars to the right-wing *American Spectator* magazine in order to dig up dirt on Bill Clinton. As a . . . non-profit organization, this money was not subject to tax. However, this money could not be used for political purposes. You can judge for yourself whether the intent was political, even if it was couched in journalistic language. Even if nobody went to jail for tax fraud for the Arkansas Project, the intent of circumventing tax laws was clearly evident.

The Project's money was used mainly to pay journalists who have admitted to lying, private investigators who engaged in shady practices and the bribery of anti-Clinton witnesses in the Whitewater [land deal investigation].

On the count of lying journalists, we have David Brock. Brock . . . recently wrote a book in which he detailed how he lied and fabricated stories in order to curry favor with the conservative elite. Arguably, Brock's most famous story was about "Troopergate," in which Arkansas state troopers were supposedly used to cover up then-Governor Clinton's sexual trysts. According to an article in the May 18, 2001, Salon.com, Brock was reimbursed to the tune of $40,000 by the Arkansas Project.

According to Brock, Ted Olson, former lawyer for the *American Spectator* and current Solicitor General of the United States, told Brock that "while he didn't place any stock in the piece, it was worth publishing because the role of the *Spectator* was to write Clinton scandal stories in hopes of 'shaking scandals loose.'"

Related to this, although not written by Brock, was "The Arkansas Drug Shuttle," an article in the *American Spectator* that alleged Clinton was involved in cocaine-running out of a small airport in Mena, Ark. According to *Crossfire*, a book written by Arkansas State Trooper L.D. Brown, he was paid $10,000 for the false story.

Sure, one can create crazy stories about Bill Clinton as much as one wants, but how can they have an impact if they're limited to a magazine like the *American Spectator*, with its admittedly small subscriber base and narrow readership? Well, the *Spectator* was read by top Republican politicians and conservative pundits, who played up the stories in interviews and television appearances. From those appearances and interviews, the mainstream media had no choice but to report on the stories they were bringing up. Therefore, the low standards of journalism at the *American Spectator* were infecting the rest of the news media . . . even though [the] incorrectness [of the stories] was easily verifiable.

Second, there are the private detectives. The May 22, 2001, Salon.com reports that the Arkansas Project paid Mississippi private detective Rex Armistead $400,000. Some of this money was involved in the harassment of CNN correspondent John Camp, who was critical of the Whitewater investigation. Armistead contacted Camp's ex-wife in search of dirt on Camp. A file on Camp also mysteriously appeared in the offices of a Republican House committee. Also asserted by Salon.com, [reporter] Joe Conason, who did much of the reporting that broke the story of the Arkansas Project, judges involved in the Whitewater prosecution who were not antagonistic enough against the Clintons were harassed by Project-funded detectives.

If real scandals could not bring him down, fake ones had to be created.

The question remains: With all the rumors that already existed about Clinton's sex life, why bother to lie and harangue innocent people in order to kick them out of office? The answer lies in a statement by someone who is involved in one of Scaife's other conservative projects. In addition to the Arkansas Project, Scaife created an organization called the Allegheny Institute for Public Policy (AIPP), a think tank in Western Pennsylvania. The AIPP's president was a man named Jerry Bowler. In a previous job as leader of the National Reform Organization, Bowler said that his goal was the creation of "Christocracy, the rule of Christ over the nation," according to an article in the May 2, 1999, *Washington Post*. Now it is clear why all this money and effort was spent on petty attacks. It is nearly limitless the extent to which people who believe that their ideas are the only ones approved by God will go. To the Arkansas Project's participants, the election of Bill Clinton was a mistake on the part of a decadent and sinful population. If real scandals could not bring him down, fake ones had to be created, all in the name of God. They are not dissimilar to the people from the conservative web forum Free Republic who vote hundreds of times in web polls in order to skew the results. Why change minds on issues when you can just stuff the ballot? Why convince people your policy proposals are good when you can insinuate that the other guy is a letch? To people like Scaife, democracy and truth are important insofar as they advance the imposition of theocracy in America.

9

The Media Suppressed the Anti–Iraq War Viewpoint

Steve Rendall and Tara Broughel

Steve Rendall is the senior analyst for Fairness and Accuracy in the Media (FAIR), cohost of CounterSpin, *FAIR's national radio show, and coauthor of* The Way Things Aren't: Rush Limbaugh's Reign of Error. *Tara Broughel is an intern at FAIR's bimonthly magazine* Extra!

In the weeks following the U.S. invasion of Iraq in March 2003, hundreds of thousands of demonstrators protested the war in cities throughout the world. The antiwar viewpoint, however, was largely absent on television news programs. Instead hundreds of prowar military and government officials dominated the discussion on network and cable news shows. Analysis of events by these guests bordered on cheerleading the U.S. efforts. Serious problems concerning death and destruction from the invasion, as well as issues of international law, human rights, and global reaction to the war were all but ignored.

Since the invasion of Iraq began in March [2003], official voices have dominated U.S. network newscasts, while opponents of the war have been notably underrepresented, according to a study by FAIR.

Starting the day after the invasion of Iraq began on March 19, the three-week study (3/20/03–4/9/03) looked at 1,617 on-camera sources appearing in stories about Iraq on the evening newscasts of six television networks and news channels. The news programs studied were *ABC World News Tonight*, *CBS Evening News*, *NBC Nightly News*, CNN's *Wolf Blitzer Reports*, Fox's *Special Report with Brit Hume*, and PBS's *NewsHour with Jim Lehrer*.

Sources were coded by name, occupation, nationality, position on the war and the network on which they appeared. Sources were categorized as having a position on the war if they expressed a policy opinion on the news shows studied, were currently affiliated with governments or institutions that took a position on the war, or otherwise took a prominent stance. For instance, retired Gen. Wesley Clark, a hired military analyst for CNN, was not categorized as pro-war; we could find no evidence he explicitly endorsed the invasion or was affiliated with a group supporting the war. However, retired Gen. Barry McCaffrey, an NBC analyst, was classified as pro-war as a board member of the Committee for a Free Iraq, a pro-war group.

Nearly two-thirds of all sources, 64 percent, were pro-war, while 71 percent of U.S. guests favored the war. Anti-war voices were 10 percent of all sources, but just 6 percent of non-Iraqi sources and only 3 percent of U.S. sources. Thus viewers were more than six times as likely to see a pro-war source as one who was anti-war; counting only U.S. guests, the ratio increases to 25 to 1.

The official story

Official voices, including current and former government employees, whether civilian or military, dominated network newscasts, accounting for 63 percent of overall sources. Current and former U.S. officials alone provided more than half (52 percent) of all sources; adding officials from Britain, chief ally in the invasion of Iraq, brought the total to 57 percent.

Looking at U.S. sources, which made up 76 percent of total sources, more than two out of three (68 percent) were either current or former officials. The percentage of U.S. sources who were officials varied from network to network, ranging from 75 percent at CBS to 60 percent at NBC.

In the category of U.S. officials, military voices overwhelmed civilians by a two-to-one margin, providing 68 percent of U.S. official sources and nearly half (47 percent) of all U.S. sources. This predominance reflected the networks' focus on information from journalists embedded with troops, or provided at military briefings, and the analysis of such by paid former military officials.

Former military personnel, who often appeared in longer-format, in-studio interviews, rather than in soundbites, characteristically offered technical commentary supportive of U.S. military efforts. In a typical comment, retired general (and CNN consultant) Wesley Clark told Wolf Blitzer on April 6: "Well, the United States has very, very important technological advantages. Unlike previous efforts in urban combat, we control the skies." Analysis by these paid military commentators often blended into cheerleading, as with Clark's comment from the same interview: "First of all, I think the troops and all the people over there, the commanders, have done an absolutely superb job, a sensational job. And I think the results speak for themselves."

Nearly two-thirds of all sources, 64 percent, were pro-war. . . . Anti-war voices were 10 percent of all sources.

Though some of these analysts criticized military planning, and were attacked for doing so by the administration and its allies, the rare criticisms were clearly motivated by a desire to see U.S. military efforts succeed. For instance, while NBC's hired analyst, retired Gen. Barry McCaffrey, said he expected the U.S. to prevail in the war, he worried that there weren't sufficient ground troops in place for an expected battle for the city of Baghdad: "We have no business taking on that mission unless we're prepared to decisively employ combat power."

Of a total of 840 U.S. sources who are current or former government or military officials, only four were identified as holding anti-war opinions—Sen. Robert Byrd (D.-W.V.), Rep. Pete Stark (D.-Calif.) and two appearances by Rep. Dennis Kucinich (D.-Ohio). Byrd was featured on PBS, with Stark and Kucinich appearing on Fox News.

Overseas viewpoints

Among British news sources, 95 percent were government or military officials; the remaining 5 percent, four individuals, were all journalists. More than a third of the British public was opposed to the war at the time of this study, according to a Guardian/ICM poll, but no British anti-war voices were carried by these six news shows.

Iraq provided the only exception to the rule that official sources dominate the news. Iraqis made 200 appearances on the news shows during the study period, but less than a third of these (32 percent) were official sources. Interviews with persons on the street made up the largest category of Iraqi sources, with 62 percent of overall Iraqi appearances. Of Iraqi persons on the street, 49 percent expressed support for the U.S. war effort, while 18 percent voiced opposition, but the format of on-the-street interviews seldom elicited deep insights from either side; typical comments included "God damn to bloody hell Saddam" (CBS) and "They can go. USA go" (Fox).

> *Given that the war was ultimately justified as being fought for the liberation of the people of Iraq, sources who represented Iraqi civil society were in remarkably short supply.*

Given that the war was ultimately justified as being fought for the liberation of the people of Iraq, sources who represented Iraqi civil society were in remarkably short supply on the news. Two of such Iraqi sources were clergymembers, one was a journalist and one represented a nongovernmental organization. Nine sources came from Iraqi militia groups, both pro- and anti-U.S.

Only 6 percent of all sources came from countries other than the U.S., Britain or Iraq. Given the strong opposition to the war measured in most countries that were not directly involved in the invasion, it's perhaps unsurprising that these sources had the most anti-war representation; 48 percent either voiced criticism or were officials of governments that criticized the war.

Citizens from those nations that most vocally opposed the U.S. war policy—France, Germany and Russia—accounted for 16 appearances, constituting just 1 percent of all guests. Nine of these 16 appearances were by government officials.

Out of 45 non-Iraqi Arab sources, a strong majority (63 percent) were opposed to the war. Kuwaitis, whose country served as a staging area for the invasion, were the only exception to this tendency; none of the eight Kuwaiti sources expressed opposition to the war.

Restricted to the street

As noted in earlier FAIR studies, overreliance on official sources leaves little room for independent policy critics or grassroots voices. At a time when dissent was quite visible in U.S. society, with large anti-war demonstrations across the country and 27 percent of the public telling pollsters they opposed the war, the networks largely ignored anti-war opinion in the U.S.

Not a single show . . . conducted a sit-down interview with a person identified as being against the war.

The FAIR study found just 3 percent of U.S. sources represented or expressed opposition to the war. With more than one in four U.S. citizens opposing the war and much higher rates of opposition in most countries where opinion was polled, none of the outlets studied offered anything resembling proportionate coverage of anti-war voices. The anti-war percentages ranged from 4 percent at NBC, 3 percent at CNN, ABC, PBS and FOX, and less than 1 percent—one out of 205 U.S. sources—at CBS.

While the percentage of Americans opposing the war was about 10 times higher in the real world as on the nightly news (27 percent versus 3 percent), their proportion of the guestlist may still *overstate* the degree to which they were able to present their views on U.S. television. Guests with anti-war viewpoints were almost universally allowed one-sentence soundbites taken from interviews conducted on the street. Not a single show in the study conducted a sit-down interview with a person identified as being against the war.

Anti-war sources were treated so fleetingly that they often weren't even quoted by name. While 80 percent of all sources appearing on the nightly news shows were identified by name, 42 percent of anti-war voices went unnamed or were labeled with such vague terms as "protester" or "anti-war activist." Only one leader of an anti-war group appeared as a source: Leslie Cagan of United for Peace and Justice, a New York–based organizer of anti-war marches, appeared on a March 27 CNN segment in a one-sentence soundbite from an on-the-street interview.

Beyond the battlefield

Perhaps as striking as the dominance of official voices and the scarcity of dissent on these shows was the absence of experts dealing in non-military issues. The story of war is much larger than simply what happens on the battlefield; it includes issues of international law, human rights and global and regional politics—issues beyond the scope and expertise of former generals.

But few people with the expertise to address such questions were sought out on the nightly news. FAIR found that academics, think-tank staffers and representatives of nongovernmental organizations (NGOs) accounted for just 4 percent of all sources.

With 64 appearances overall, this group included just one source who spoke against the war, Rev. Al Sharpton of the National Action Center, a civil rights NGO. Twelve sources supported the war, while the remaining 51 sources did not take an explicit position.

Nearly half of the think-tank sources (seven of 16) favored the war, while none opposed. The Council on Foreign Relations was the most frequently represented; two of its three sources supported the war. Academic sources included three supporters of the war and no opponents.

The International Committee of the Red Cross, which takes no political positions, was the leading NGO, with four appearances; no other NGO had more than one appearance. Of those with discernable positions on the war, two sources were in favor, one opposed.

More often, when television wanted a non-official source to provide context, it turned, somewhat incestuously, to journalists from other news outlets—who provided 8 percent of all sources. Relatives of military personnel made up another 4 percent of sources.

10

ABC News Was Biased Against the U.S. War in Iraq

Tim Graham

Tim Graham is the director of media analysis for the Media Research Center, an organization that opposes liberal media bias. He has served as White House correspondent for World, *a national weekly Christian newsmagazine, and is the author of the book* Pattern of Deception: The Media's Role in the Clinton Presidency.

While covering the events that led up to the Iraq war in March 2003, ABC's evening news show, *World News Tonight*, tilted dramatically to the left. Compared to *CBS Evening News* and the *NBC Nightly News*, ABC's anchorman Peter Jennings demonstrated a liberal bias. He often questioned the Bush administration's motives for war while ignoring the atrocities committed by Saddam Hussein's regime. In addition, *World News Tonight* repeated propagandistic statements from Hussein without investigating their accuracy or treating them with skepticism. While a majority of Americans supported the invasion, Jennings often suggested that the war was unjustified and unnecessary.

In times of war, the media grow skeptical of the American government's role in controlling the flow of information. But the American people are also concerned about the media's control of the flow of information. Will they act as neutral observers, devoted to balance and accuracy? Or will they play an activist's role in undermining our government's effectiveness in waging war?

During a January 17 [2003] *Nightline/Viewpoint* special, ABC News President David Westin explained why he banned the wearing of flag pins by his reporters: "I think our patriotic duty as journalists in the United States is to try to be independent and objective and present the facts to the American people and let them decide all the important things. . . . I respect any other news organization taking a different tack, but for me, part of the symbolism of the fact that what we're doing in our constitutional democracy, what we're trying to do to help quote, 'the cause of the country overall,' is to be objective and give just the straight facts to the American people and let them decide what they want to do about it."

In a review of 234 stories on ABC's *World News Tonight* from January 1 to March 7, the Media Research Center found that ABC News failed its promise to serve the American people as an independent and objective observer, offering straight facts and letting the people decide. Instead, ABC employed a dangerous double standard—harshly criticizing of the Bush administration and its policies, but failing to extend that same tough critical standard to other actors in this political crisis, from congressional Democrats, to United Nations [UN] bureaucrats, to skeptical allies like France, and even to the dictatorship in Iraq.

ABC News failed its promise to serve the American people as an independent and objective observer.

CBS Evening News and *NBC Nightly News* presented a more balanced and less passionate evaluation of news developments. *World News Tonight* coverage of the crucial pre-war debate demonstrated a clear and repetitive bias on four fronts:

• ABC questioned the purity of the Bush administration's ideological and economic motives for war, and constantly decried a lack of White House respect for the peacemaking efforts of countries like France and the United Nations. ABC did not apply the same skeptical standards on ideology, greed, or "hard line" demands when it came to the policy stands of France or the United Nations.

• While ABC treated Bush administration pronouncements with great skepticism, ABC routinely channeled propaganda from the Iraqi regime without investigating its accuracy or even treating it with equal skepticism.

• ABC has touted the size and broadly "mainstream" nature of anti-war protest movements, without skeptical coverage of their radical organizers, their radical speeches, or their potentially destructive impact on the popularity of the "peace" position.

• ABC selectively covered its own polling numbers, reporting results that show slippage for the White House case, while sometimes ignoring its own polls when they found growing support for the White House case.

While the American public grow more convinced every day of the need for war, they have not arrived at that opinion through objective reporting from ABC that demonstrated faith in letting the American people decide for themselves. Instead, ABC's coverage on *World News Tonight* has scorned the notion of balance, lobbying the American people by favoring and highlighting information suggesting that war is unjustified, unnecessary, undiplomatic, and unwise.

Championing France and the United Nations over the U.S.

Throughout his months of presiding over pre-war *World News Tonight* coverage, ABC anchor Peter Jennings has projected the impression that his role is to accentuate all the negatives to slow down the "rush to war," and put America's impulsive militarism under the yoke of UN and French reasonableness. Every UN and ally's objection was not a position to be debated, but a "problem" to be solved, presumably through a prolonged period of surrendering to further diplomatic delays. . . .

The White House cites UN resolutions to argue Iraq is the party obligated to demonstrate that it has rid itself of weapons of mass destruction, and the burden is not on the U.S. or the UN inspectors to find fresh proof of improper weapons within Iraq. But Jennings began on January 9 with an on-screen graphic reading "UN weapons inspectors find no 'smoking guns,'" and a verbal focus on White House problems: "We're going to begin with problems for the Bush administration if it really wants to overthrow Saddam Hussein militarily. United Nations weapons inspectors have said today they are not finding evidence that Iraq has weapons of mass destruction. And the administration's most loyal supporter for military action, the British Prime Minister, says Mr. Bush should not rush things."

As the momentum toward war picked up on February 7, Jennings introduced another story with the usual hard foot on the brakes: "Now to the Bush administration's campaign against Iraq. Just as the Iraqis appear to be making some concessions, the U.S. thinks it has growing support for war." The White House "thinks" it had growing support? As shown later in this report, ABC's own polls at that time showed growing support after Colin Powell presented evidence of Iraqi deceit to the UN.

Jaded Jennings ended the program on a note of cynicism: "Finally this evening, some notes about things to keep an eye on. The UN weapons inspectors go back to Baghdad this weekend. They have not been happy with Iraqi cooperation so far. We'll see if the Iraqis do any better—and if that means anything to the Bush administration."

In live coverage of the UN debate on February 14, the primary Jennings complaint was American non-cooperation, not Iraqi non-cooperation. Jennings painted President Bush, not France, as the impediment to allied unity: "Terry Moran, as you look at this from the distance at least of being on the road, and I think a lot of people got the impression this week that maybe the Bush administration doesn't mind if the Western alliance as we've known it in the post-war period breaks up. Some people are puzzled by that." A few hours later, Jennings flipped back again to how Bush alone is threatening to crumble the alliance: "What's happening here . . . is an effort in the Security Council among allies, remember, for the most part, to go forward together and not rupture this, or any other international body to which they all belong. And yet the Bush administration is determined to have its way on this."

Blaming the White House

On February 19, when the White House expressed hopes for a "second" resolution to underline the need for military action, CBS's Dan Rather and NBC's Tom Brokaw managed to launch their newscasts without heavy-handed rebukes.

Brokaw led off from Kuwait: "Countdown Iraq. The U.S. will bring a new war resolution to a vote at the UN, President Bush calls it 'the last chance.'"

Also from Kuwait, Dan Rather announced at the top of the *Evening News:* "With the timetable for a possible new war with Iraq slipping, the United States is pushing for the United Nations Security Council to give Saddam Hussein a flat deadline for disarming. The White House said it will offer a draft resolution this week or next."

Compare that to how Peter Jennings approached the Bush policy on Iraq, assuming it's the Bush team, not a few allies, which deserved low marks on playing well with others. "It is quite clear in Washington tonight that the administration is prepared to jeopardize its relations with several of its oldest and best friends in order to get its way about Iraq."

A journalist could have suggested "old Europe" was jeopardizing relations, perhaps even with economic motivations of trading partnerships with [Saddam Hussein's] Baathist regime. But not at ABC. White House reporter Terry Moran brought the usual Bush-the-cowboy approach: "With nearly 200,000 U.S. troops now in the Persian Gulf, the White House today presented what amounted to an ultimatum to the fourteen other nations on the Security Council."

On February 27, CBS's John Roberts and NBC's Andrea Mitchell both noted how the UN Security Council's debate over Iraq grew "bitter," but both refrained from blaming any one party. ABC's Terry Moran once again blamed the White House: "At the UN Security Council today, the Bush administration's hard line contributed to what diplomats said was an unusually bitter debate that yielded no consensus and left smaller nations feeling intense pressure from both the U.S. and France."

Why does the U.S. have a "hard line," but not France? France argued that it would veto any resolution, regardless of the language, if it authorizes military action. That's not a hard line? Not at ABC. . . .

UN motives rarely scrutinized

While the United States was arrogant and uncompromising, the statements and actions of United Nations personnel and allied ministers of state were rarely scrutinized by ABC. On January 27, CBS's Dan Rather and NBC's Tom Brokaw both noted the UN arms inspectors found no "smoking gun," but both led their newscasts by stressing how Iraq has failed to comply with the UN resolution.

Rather led off his broadcast: "Tonight's headlines: Chief inspector slams Iraq. U.S. says time is almost up."

Brokaw began his show: "Road to War: UN weapons inspectors say Saddam is not coming clean. They want more time."

On ABC, Peter Jennings opened with a milder tone: "On *World News Tonight,* the United Nations inspectors say Iraq has not yet accepted that it must disarm. The inspectors want more time to do their job." Jennings stressed how the nuclear inspector, Mohamed el-Baradei, was much softer on Iraq, a point of view CBS and NBC treated as a minor detail later in their broadcasts. Jennings announced that el-Baradei "said they have found no evidence of a nuclear weapons program so far and, his words now, 'provided there is sustained proactive cooperation by Iraq, we should be able within the next few months to provide credible assurance that Iraq has no nuclear weapons program.'"

Jennings also treated the reaction to the UN report from the White

House and Saddam's minions as equally credible: "After spending last week in Baghdad listening to the Iraqi government, what we heard from the Iraqi government today is also as it was at the White House: true to form." From Baghdad, ABC's Dan Harris repeated that the Iraqi regime claimed "they have exhibited not only cooperation, but quote, 'super-cooperation.' Iraqi officials said the only way to avoid hostilities now is for the U.S. to stop its threats and warmongering."

Jennings interviewed Secretary of State Colin Powell and hit him repeatedly from the left.

When [chief UN weapons inspector] Hans Blix presented a report to the Security Council on February 14 attempting to soft-pedal Iraqi violations, Jennings opened that evening's *World News Tonight:* "The UN weapons inspectors have given their latest report on Iraq to the United Nations Security Council, and once again it brings into focus a lack of consensus on attacking Iraq. The Bush administration had hoped that the weapons inspectors would be very hard on Iraq today for not coming clean about weapons of mass destruction. It didn't work out precisely like that. And even with some of its allies, the administration did not have its best day." On this evening, CBS and NBC were equally negative about White House hopes.

But Jennings then presented a paper decree from Saddam as "another concession," as if Iraq is continually cooperating: "Not long before Mr. Blix briefed the Security Council, the Iraqis announced another concession. Saddam Hussein issued a presidential decree banning the production or the importation of chemical, biological and nuclear weapons, and all of the materials used to make them. This is something the inspectors have been requesting for a decade." CBS reporter Mark Phillips at least added, "It's a legal ban not likely to satisfy those who think he still has them."

Earlier that day, all the networks presented the UN proceedings live, but ABC emerged as the least eager to describe Iraqi non-cooperation.

On CBS, Dan Rather declared his headline: "Hans Blix said today that Iraq has failed to account for many proscribed weapons and must still explain what happened to suspected stocks of anthrax, VX gas, and long-range missiles."

On NBC, Andrea Mitchell reported: "He did find what you could call a smoking gun, which is that one of the missiles, the al-Samoud missile, as we reported last night, is longer than the range permitted. It is 113 miles rather than 90 miles."

But Jennings summed up with vagueness: "On the one hand it's better, on the one hand it could be better, on the one hand he argues for a little longer time. On the other hand he says it depends on the Security Council, it certainly depends on the United States, which has not much interest in giving the weapons inspectors any time."

A few minutes after Terry Moran described the Bush team's "ultimatum" to allies on February 19, ABC's Dan Harris in Baghdad went a little easier on Iraq: "In recent days, Saddam Hussein has met many of the weapons inspectors' key demands. . . . In fact, the chief inspectors have said they've seen the beginnings of a change of attitude. However, on closer inspection, there is less to Iraq's cooperation than meets the eye." Harris noted whose attitude leads to Iraqi non-cooperation: "Tonight one top Iraqi official hinted at why the government may not be feeling much pressure to act. He said given the huge international peace protests and the growing anti-war sentiment at the UN, it is America that is in trouble." If America was "in trouble," ABC would easily qualify as one of national media's leading troublemakers.

On March 7, Jennings interviewed Secretary of State Colin Powell and hit him repeatedly from the left on the great utility of the inspectors: "So many people don't understand why you shouldn't let the inspections continue if they are accomplishing anything?" He followed up: "Most people think they're doing a reasonably effective job at the moment." He also accused Powell of "moving the goalpost . . . so the Security Council is left in the position of either agreeing with you completely or else."

Channeling Iraqi propaganda

While the White House was presented as a bull in a china shop, ABC often presented Saddam Hussein's regime as . . . exactly the way Saddam wanted it presented. Reporting from Baghdad on January 21, Jennings told White House reporter Terry Moran, "it looks from here, maybe it looks from everywhere, that Mr. Bush is more and more determined to attack the Iraqis." Jennings soon decided that "when Saddam Hussein looks out from here, he also sees many of America's allies saying that President Bush is in too much of a hurry to go to war."

That evening, the first few seconds of the network news displayed yet another contrast between the Big Three, with ABC coming in softest.

CBS Evening News anchor Dan Rather began the show "Tonight's headlines: Another terror attack on Americans in the Gulf."

On *NBC Nightly News*, Tom Brokaw opened: "Showdown over Iraq: President Bush aims tough words at Saddam Hussein and also at U.S. allies who want more time."

On ABC, Jennings began with the public-relations benefits for Saddam: "On World News Tonight this Tuesday, President Bush says there are no options left: Saddam Hussein is facing war. The administration says it will go it alone if need be. . . . An American killed in Kuwait: Anti-Americanism in the region may be a comfort to Saddam Hussein." He not only claimed inaccurately that Bush would "go it alone," the first words out of his mouth did not include "terrorism." It was just "anti-Americanism" that made Saddam's day.

But the real eye-opener that night came when the anchorman wrapped up with a celebration of Iraqi arts and letters: "For many years now, the United States and most Americans have looked at Iraq and tended to see only its dictator. But this is a country with a very long history of, among other things, arts and letters. This week we were surprised to see several hundred artists and writers walking through the streets of Baghdad to say thank you to Saddam Hussein. He had just increased their monthly financial support. Cynical, you could argue with this particular time, but the state has always supported the arts, and some of the most creative people in the Arab world have always been Iraqis. And whatever they think about Saddam Hussein in the privacy of their homes, on this occasion they were praising his defense of the homeland in the face of American threats."

Why would Jennings be "surprised" at Iraqi subjects being paraded before his eyes as their monthly checks arrived? And why would he do the Iraqi regime the favor of displaying this cynical parade as he dismissed its human props and "whatever they think . . . in the privacy of their homes"? . . .

ABC's Dan Harris created another Baghdad blast of anti-war hype, underlining how a U.S. invasion will kill children and cause massive miscarriages.

ABC even went the extra mile of anticipating Iraqi propaganda lines and advancing them before they could be concocted. After live coverage of the State of the Union address and the Democratic response on January 28, Jennings called on reporter Dan Harris in Baghdad who called President Bush's charge that Iraq is not cooperating with inspectors "low hanging fruit" for them to dismiss:

> When the leadership of this country wakes up in a couple of hours, the sun is just coming up right now, I suspect they will latch on to many of the complaints we've heard from President Bush tonight. Most notably I think the low hanging fruit is this idea that they're still hiding weapons of mass destruction. They'll point out that the inspectors have been here for more than 60 days and have so far found nothing. I think you'll also hear a reaction to this idea that President Bush put forward of liberating Iraq. Saddam Hussein was on TV a couple of hours ago saying the Americans want to enslave Iraq.

This was one of those moments where viewers might wonder: If reporters truthfully despise being "stenographers to power," how can they stand in Baghdad and not only act as stenographers for tyrants, but go so far as to compose their next set of talking points while they sleep? CBS and NBC coverage also featured reaction pieces from their reporters in Iraq, but CBS's Elizabeth Palmer and NBC's Ron Allen refrained from so generously relaying potential enemy propaganda lines. They focused on how Iraqi citizens may or may not hear what Bush said and how Iraq responded to the latest UN report.

"Human shields"

Another Iraqi propaganda ploy was loosening its migration standards for so-called "human shields," left-wing activists who pledged to stand in front of civilian targets and risk death to keep the war from happening. On the February 26 *World News Tonight*, Baghdad-based Dan Harris trumpeted the cause of one such American. "Ryan Clancy, a substitute English teacher from Milwaukee, became so convinced that a war with Iraq would be unjustified and unwise that he sold his stake in a local record store and came to Baghdad where he just moved into a food storage facility to act as a human shield. . . . He says the goal of the human shields is to stop the war, or at the very least, to stop the U.S. from bombing sites vital to Iraqi civilians." Harris allowed that Defense Secretary Donald Rumsfeld suggested that placing innocent civilians around likely bombing targets is a war crime, but he also rebutted: "But human rights lawyers say if the Pentagon bombs places inhabited by human shields, that too would be a war crime."

Harris toyed around with the obvious point: "The human shields themselves are facing a problem as well: how to avoid being tools of the Iraqi government, which is paying for their transportation and their housing, including stocked refrigerators." He didn't find a spokesman to expand on that little "problem," but simply concluded with stenography for Ryan Clancy: "He says he's not here to protect Saddam Hussein, just the Iraqi people."

CBS and NBC both offered more skeptical coverage of these Saddam-assisted publicity stunt specialists. The night before Harris's report, Dan Rather briefly profiled Ryan Clancy on *CBS Evening News*, mentioning "he's left one troubled family behind." While his mother was scared but proud, Clancy said his father "accused me of siding with the enemy and pretty much called me a terrorist." The next night, as Harris puffed Clancy on ABC, CBS reporter David Martin suggested "Saddam is bringing in anti-war activists to serve as human shields and placing more and more military equipment near religious and civilian targets" to "complicate American battle plans."

NBC Nightly News didn't profile "shields" until March 4, but they also had a more balanced story than ABC. Reporter Kevin Tibbles found: "There are about fifty Americans already in Iraq, representing various groups and religious organizations working to prevent war. But to many other Americans, acting as a human shield is both foolish and unpatriotic." Tibbles balanced that critical viewpoint from David Riddell, whose brother Sean is a Marine, with rebuttals from his aunt Michele Riddell, who is a "human shield.". . .

On February 28, ABC's Dan Harris created another Baghdad blast of anti-war hype, underlining how a U.S. invasion will kill children and cause massive miscarriages. He began by emphasizing the regime's focus on normality. As viewers saw video of a couple getting married and crowded streets with people out shopping, Harris reported over video of Saddam and his soldiers: "Even from Saddam Hussein there's a measure of public levity. . . . On Iraqi TV recently one of his soldiers told him a joke, something about a married couple. 'That's a good one,' said the President."

Harris then shifted to growing anxiety: "The government has given people six months worth of food rations. People are digging wells in their backyards, and hospitals, including this maternity hospital, are bracing for war." A nurse then predicted in English: "For sure there'll be premature labors and for sure there'll be high percentage of miscarriages, for sure it will be like that." Then Harris shifted to "Iraq's youngest citizens," as interviewed by Norwegian child psychologist and "peace" activist Magne Raundalen. Dr. Raundalen asked children: "If there was an attack, what would that mean?" Harris concluded the story by relaying one child's answer: "'They will attack us by airplanes and missiles and guns,' he says. His brother says 'a great number of people, especially children, will die.'"

Even as the time for war drew near in March, ABC kept pressing the Iraqi talking points about their great compliance efforts, as if they came straight from Saddam stooge [Foreign Minister] Tariq Aziz. Jennings set up a March 4 story from Dan Harris in Baghdad: "In Iraq today, while the Iraqis continue to comply with the UN weapons inspectors, the Iraqi President, Saddam Hussein, was attacking the United States in a public letter to Iraqis.". . .

Recommendations for improved coverage

Reporters should seek a balance of arguments and a balance of skepticism in covering both the United States and allies and international organizations. The American people should expect skepticism in coverage of the White House, but they also expect skepticism in presenting the United Nations and difficult allies like France. All of these actors played a crucial role in the pre-war debate, and merited journalistic skepticism of their positions, motives, and in the case of the UN, their ability to function as a cohesive organization.

Untrustworthy enemy claims should not be given equal weight with the statements of American officials. The free American media should be extremely dubious of the self-serving claims of an enemy dictatorship. Journalists are at their worst when they hammer away at the legitimacy of the government which grants them their freedoms at the same time they're presenting credulous Potemkin-village propaganda reports from a dictatorship. At the bare minimum, U.S. and Iraqi claims should be submitted to a similar acid test of truthfulness.

11

Iraq War Coverage Was Orchestrated by the White House.

Danny Schechter

Danny Schechter is a critic and author of The More You Watch the Less You Know, News Dissector, *and several other books on the media.*

When the United States invaded Iraq in March 2003, the White House used media professionals to portray President Bush and U.S. military commanders in the most flattering light on television. Reporters were "embedded," or allowed to travel with U.S. fighting troops on condition that they provide patriotic images and human interest stories and not show dead bodies or other destruction to viewers back home. By managing the willing media, the White House was able to use newspapers, magazines, and television and radio programs to promote its political interests while silencing its critics. While this tactic may have benefited the political aspirations of the president and the financial concerns of media conglomerates, it denied the truth about the war to the American public.

Few of us escaped seeing the non-stop reports from Iraq from journalists—embedded and otherwise—on what have been described as the front lines of the fight for "Iraqi freedom." Throughout the American media world, and beyond, there has been a hearty sense of a job well done, except of course, for regrets over those colleagues and soldiers who never made it home. We all watched the war as if it was only a military conflict. It wasn't. There was also a carefully planned, tightly controlled and brilliantly executed media war that was fought alongside it. For the most part, that other media war was not covered or fully explained, even though it was right in front of us.

The Baghdad-based reporters who worked under limitations imposed by the now defunct Iraqi Ministry of Information were not shy about telling us what they had to put up with. When that ministry and the TV station it managed were "taken out" [by the United States] in bombing attacks that flouted international laws, American newscasters cheered. Its propaganda function was crude and obvious. However, there was also propaganda flowing from other regional media aimed at the "Arab street," which also was crude and distorted. While [Arab] outlets like *Al-Jazeera* and Abu Dhabi TV strived to offer professional reporting, which in some instances out-scooped Western networks, other commentary reflected longstanding cultural biases—anti-Americanism, inflammatory anti-Semitism—with loads of violence and no attention paid to Saddam Hussein's human rights abuses or to women's rights. Kurdish journalists, who lived under the impact of Saddam's ethnic cleansing in the north, criticized Arab satellite stations for these serious shortcomings.

Many U.S. newscasts pointed to these flaws and biases in part to project their own work as being free of similar problems. "They"—the "other"—practiced propaganda common to backward societies. We, of the developed world, practiced world-class, bias-free journalism—or so we wanted the world to believe.

Americans . . . have been subjected to a propaganda barrage in an effort to neutralize opposition to the war.

The truth is that there were pervasive Western propaganda techniques built into American media presentation formats and many were highly sophisticated. Others obvious. They were rarely commented on or critiqued, except by war critics. Few journalists reported fully on their own government's propaganda campaign and its interface with their own products. Washington's anti-Iraqi propaganda was multidimensional and a key component of the "coalition" war plan. (Deceptive words like "coalition" were themselves part of it.) Aimed at the Iraqis was a well-crafted arsenal of psychological operations, or Psy-Ops, carried out by [a United States] IO (Information Operations) directorate that simultaneously targeted and destroyed the country's communication system and replaced it with its own. A second front—and perhaps a more important one—was the Western public. Iraqis were targeted by bombs and information warfare while Western audiences had a well executed propaganda campaign often posing as news directed their way. British-based propaganda expert Paul de Rooij explains in several well-sourced assessments, "One generally doesn't think of psychological warfare as something waged against the home population; but this is perhaps the best way to appreciate the U.S. experience during the past few months. The objective of such a campaign was to stifle dissent, garner unquestioning support, and rally people around a common symbol. Americans, and to a lesser extent Europeans, have been subjected to a propaganda barrage in an effort to neutralize opposition to the war, and this fits directly into a psy-ops framework." All the networks had platoons of retired generals and pro-war military experts interpreting war news. U.S. TV quickly resembled Chilean TV after the coup. One Canadian critic called U.S. network, "the Pentagon's bitch." CNN's news chief Eason Jordan revealed that he had sought approval from the Pentagon for his network's key war advisors. At war's end, critic Michael Moore rightly demanded the "unilateral withdrawal of the Pentagon from America's TV studios."

War as a political campaign

Pentagon media chief Tori Clarke, who worked with PR firms and political campaigns before bringing a corporate approach and politically oriented spin operation into the Pentagon, admitted that she was running her shop the way she used to run campaigns. This approach was coordinated throughout the Administration with "messages of the day" and orchestrated appearances by the president and members of his cabinet. They were not just selling a message, but "managing the perceptions" of those who received them. In political outage, they used "stagecraft," a term that once was used to refer to covert operations.

On May 16, 2003, the *New York Times* detailed how the Bush administration relies on TV entertainment techniques to sell the president and his policies. [Reporter] Elisabeth Bumiller wrote: "Officials of past Democratic and Republican administrations marvel at how the White House does not seem to miss an opportunity to showcase Mr. Bush in dramatic and perfectly lighted settings. It is all by design: the White House has stocked its communications operation with people from network television who have expertise in lighting, camera angles, and the importance of backdrops.

We no longer live in a traditional democracy but, rather, a media-ocracy, a land in which media, the military, and politics fuse.

"TV news people have been tapped in this aspect of the media war. First among equals is Scott Sforza, a former ABC producer who was hired by the Bush campaign in Austin, Texas, and who now works for Dan Bartlett, the White House communications director. Sforza created the White House message of the day backdrops and helped design the $250,000 set at the United States Central Command forward headquarters in Doha, Qatar, during the Iraq war. Sforza works closely with Bob DeServi, a former NBC cameraperson whom the Bush White House hired after seeing his work in the 2000 campaign. DeServi, whose title is associate director of communications for production, is considered a master at lighting."

A third crucial player is Greg Jenkins, a former Fox News television producer in Washington, Bumiller revealed. These smartly polished sales techniques worked and typified the way the war was sold—and covered. It all underscores once again that we no longer live in a traditional democracy but, rather, a media-ocracy, a land in which media, the military, and politics fuse. *New York Times* columnist Paul Krugman, who has written about how media coverage shapes public opinion, makes another point about the way TV coverage distorts reality. "The administration's anti-terror campaign makes me think of the way television studios really look. The fancy set usually sits in the middle of a shabby room full of cardboard and duct tape. Networks take great care with what viewers see on their TV screens; they spend as little as possible on anything off camera. And so it has been with the campaign against terrorism. Bush strikes heroic poses on TV, but his administration neglects anything that isn't photogenic," Krugman wrote. No wonder we had newscasts in which images trumped information.

War as a TV show

This war was a TV show on a new scale with as many "events" as a televised Olympics. Media outlets were willing, even enthusiastic participants in a made-for-television spectacle. It would be wrong and overly deterministic to conclude that these TV news operations were taken over, duped, or manipulated by the kind of crude force that prevails in some other countries between government agencies and the media. The Pentagon was not faxing instructions to the newsrooms, nor would they have to. Media companies had their own reasons for playing the role they did, as did "yellow press" publisher William Randolph Hearst who [in the early twentieth century] used—and, many say, started—war as a way to sell papers. He is reported to have said, "You furnish the pictures and I'll furnish the war" at the beginning of the Spanish-American War. Today the relationship between government and media is more symbiotic, even synergistic. Wars like the one in Iraq are staged to project American power to the world. The pictures advertise that power (and market weapons systems [to foreign buyers] at the same time). The news business is more than happy to oblige because war attracts viewers in large numbers. Journalists quickly become intoxicated by the ether of war and all the excitement and danger that awaits on the front line. For many reporters, war is where the action is. It is also a career builder. Covering war has always been a way for journalists to prove their bona fides, win bragging rights, and, of course, move up the ladder in the corporate news world. War represents the highest form of professional calling and appeals to their sense of patriotism and pride. Many promote the mission of those they cover as their own, just as many beat reporters are often co-opted by the officials and the agencies on which they report. The seduction is subtle. Some may be bought as intelligence assets, but most would resent any suggestion that they have sold out—or sold in.

Networks love war. It offers riveting reality programming.

Networks love war. It offers riveting reality programming. They see it as "militainment," to borrow a term from *Time Magazine*. Its life and death drama brings in viewers and holds attention. The spectacle builds ratings and revenues. It also imbues news organizations with a sense of importance. It allows executives to demonstrate how valuable they are to the national interest. Executives at MSNBC boasted of how their war coverage brought Americans together and "emphasized the positive, not the negative." Positive coverage also helps networks gain more access to the powerful, satisfying their advertisers in an industry where three out of every 4 commercials are bought by the 50 most powerful companies. In 2003, pleasing the Bush administration also promised an economic benefit, since while the war was being waged, media companies were lobbying for regulatory changes that would benefit their bottom lines. FCC [Federal Communications Commission] chairperson Michael Powell, son of the Secretary of State [Colin Powell], who was promoting the war policy, rationalized the need for more media consolidation, in part, on grounds that only big media companies could afford to cover future wars the way this one was being covered.

Embedded reporters

Clearly, there was a campaign in this war, as in others, that involved co-opting and orchestrating the news media. The most visible center of this strategy was the effort to embed reporters. Their work was subsidized by the Pentagon, overseen by "public affairs" specialists, and linked to TV news networks dominated by military experts approved by the Pentagon. When the war was over, Rem Rieder, the editor of the *American Journalism Review (AJR)*, gushed, "It is clear that the great embedding experiment was a home run as far as the news media and the American people are concerned." General Tommy Franks agreed and pledged that embedding would be used in future conflicts. *AJR* writer Sherry Ricchiardi amplified the view most favored by the mainstream media organizations that participated in the embedding experiment, ". . . despite initial skepticism about how well the system would work and some dead-on criticism of overly enthusiastic reporting in the war's early stages, the net result was a far more complete mosaic of the fighting—replete with heroism, tragedy and human error—than would have been possible without it." She quotes Sandy Johnson, the Associated Press' Washington bureau chief, who directed coverage of the 1991 Persian Gulf War. "Compared with the scant access allowed then," Johnson says, "this system has worked incredibly well. The naysayers," she adds, "will be eating their words."

Will we? Most embedded reporters claimed that they were not really restrained, but rather assisted in their work by Pentagon press flacks. This is probably true—and the reason the system worked so well. Manipulation in a carefully calibrated media spin operation is always more insidious when the manipulated do not fully recognize how they are being used.

Many of the "embeds" acknowledged that they came to identify with and sometimes befriend the soldiers in the units they tagged along with, usually with the caveat that it was no different from covering any beat. Former TV reporter Michael Burton offered a different view of embedding: "The idea originated with the Pentagon, where military and political strategists pitched the idea to editors . . . as a compromise. The Pentagon strategists, already planning for the Iraqi war, wanted proud, positive, and patriotic coverage over the national airwaves. If the editors agreed to all their provisions for security reviews, flagging of sensitive information, limitations on filming dead bodies, and other restrictions, then journalists would be welcome. The editors went along and accepted the ground rules without a fight. Now, the story of war is seen through the eyes of the American battalions, but without the real violence. American children see more images of violence on nightly television than they do in this war, because of the deliberate editing at home. Instead, they see a fascination with high tech weapons, battle tactics, and military strategy reporting," Burton says. He claims this leads to bias, although he acknowledges that many of his former colleagues demur. "Some reporters disagree, saying that eating, sleeping, and living with the U.S. troops does not make them biased (in spite of the constant descriptions of 'we' and 'us' when reporters talk about the military units). They say they are revealing more human-interest stories in real-time."

But, while embedded journalism provides more opportunity for human interest, it only does so from the American military's perspective. Veteran *New York Times* war reporter Chris Hedges seems to agree with this view. He told *Editor & Publisher* magazine that he preferred print reporting to the TV coverage, but said that both were deeply flawed. "Print is doing a better job than TV," he observes. "The broadcast media display all these retired generals and charts and graphs, it looks like a giant game of Risk [the board game]. I find it nauseating." But even the print embeds have little choice, but to "look at Iraq totally through the eyes of the U.S. military," Hedges points out. "That's a very distorted and self-serving view."

The Project on Excellence in Journalism studied the early coverage and found that half the embedded journalists showed combat action, but not a single story depicted people hit by weapons. There were no reporters embedded with Iraqi families. None stationed with humanitarian agencies or the anti-war groups that had brought more than 15 million people on the streets before the war in a historically unprecedented display of global public opinion. The cumulative impact of the embedded reporters' work prompted former Pentagon press chief Kenneth Bacon to tell the *Wall Street Journal*, "They couldn't hire actors to do as good a job as they have done for the military."

War as sport

They were actors in a news drama that had all the earmarks of a sporting event. In fact it seems to be designed as one. The main advantage of this approach is that Americans are very comfortable with the sport show—it is part of their daily diet, it is intelligible to them, and it gives them a passive "entertained" role. When one watches a sports game, there is no need to think about the why of anything; it is only an issue of supporting our team. The play-by-play military analysts incorporated the sports analogy completely—with maps/diagrams, advice to players, and by making the audience think about the strategy.

Many of the cable news networks pictured Iraq as if it was the property of, and indistinguishable from, one mad person. Accordingly, attention was focused endlessly on where Saddam was, was he alive or dead, etc. Few references were made to U.S. dealings with his government in the 1980s or the covert role the CIA played in his rise to power. Saddam was as demonized in 2003 as Osama bin Laden had been in 2001, with news being structured as a patriotically correct morality soap opera with disinterested good guys (us) battling the forces of evil (them/him) in a political conflict constructed by the White House along "you are either with us or against us" lines. Few explained that there had been an undeclared war [of bombings and economic sanctions] in effect for more than a decade against Iraq before the hot war of 2003 was launched.

There were many stories in this war but most followed a story line that reduced the terms of coverage to two sides, the forces of light versus the forces of darkness. This is typical of all war propaganda. This war was presented on one side, the "good side," by endless CENTCOM [Central Command] military briefings, Pentagon press conferences, Ari Fleischer White House [spokesman] Q&As, Administration domination of the Sunday TV talk shows, and occasional presidential utterances riddled with religious references. Counter-posed on the other side—the "bad side"—were the crude press conferences of Iraq's hapless minister of misinformation, a cartoon figure whom no one took seriously. The two armies were spoken of as if there was some parity between their capacities. There was endless focus on the anticipated chemical or biological weapons attacks that never came and on the weapons of mass destruction that have yet to be found (at this writing).

> *American children see more images of violence on nightly television than they do in this war, because of the deliberate editing at home.*

Omitted from the picture and the reportage were views that offered any persuasive counternarrative. There were few interviews with Iraqis or experts not affiliated with pro-Administration think tanks. Or with military people, other than high-ranking retired military officials who quibbled over tactics not policy. Or with peace activists, European journalists, and, until late in the day, Arab journalists. We saw images from Al-Jazeera, but rarely heard its analysis. This list of what was left out is endless. Footage was sanitized, "breaking news" was often inaccurate, and critical voices were omitted as "Fox News" played up martial music and MSNBC ran promos urging "God Bless America." The role of "Fox News," an unabashed 24-hour booster of the war, probably deserves a book of its own. Its aggressive coverage pandered to the audience, simplified the issues, and attacked competing media outlets and correspondents who deviated in any way from the "script" they were promoting. Fox's apparent success in attracting viewers with its non-stop hawkish narrative led to a "Fox Effect" that caused many competitors to try to emulate its approach. MSNBC was accused of trying to "outfox Fox." Its coverage polarized the media war and bullied war critics.

Not everyone who watched bought into its terms or was persuaded by its story line. The war and its coverage also turned off and tuned out tens of millions who took to the streets, rejecting the pro-war media frame in the largest global protests in history. Relying on independent media, international newspapers, and websites for their information, they criticized both the policy and the press. In the aftermath of the giant February 15, 2003, protests, the *New York Times* commented that there were then two opposing global superpowers—the military might of the United States and world public opinion.

As the war erupted, the critics were "disappeared" from media view just as Saddam disposed of his critics. He used violence; our media used inattention. Even as those protests were often badly—and in some cases barely—covered, they nevertheless spoke for millions who rejected the media war aimed at their minds and spirits. One can only hope that, as the claims and "evidence" used to stoke up the war are unmasked, the media role will also be seen for what it is. As [war critic] Paul Krugman commented on the *Times* Op-ed page: "Over the last two years we've become accustomed to the pattern. Each time the Administration comes up with another whopper, partisan supporters (a group that includes a large segment of the news media) obediently insist that black is white and up is down. Meanwhile, the liberal media report only that some people say that black is black and up is up. Some Democratic politicians offer the Administration invaluable cover by making excuses and playing down the extent of their lies."

Most of us were not on the battlefield. Our understanding of what happened, our perceptions, points of view, and prejudices were forged and framed by our media choices. We need to see that as a problem that demands to be addressed. Just as we consider politicians lying to us a problem.

12

The Media Are Biased Against Gun Rights Advocates

John R. Lott Jr.

John R. Lott Jr. has published more than ninety articles in academic journals and is the author of several books about crime, guns, and gun control laws. He was a senior research scholar at Yale University's School of Law and has held positions at the University of Chicago, Stanford University, UCLA, the Wharton Business School, and Rice University.

According to some studies, the widespread ownership of guns in the United States has actually made the country safer. In fact, it is estimated that every year over 2 million crimes are prevented by law-abiding citizens who brandish guns at would-be attackers. However, news stories concerning guns omit this statistic. Newspapers, magazines, and especially TV news shows run thousands of stories in which guns are used to murder while never mentioning that guns are more often used in self-defense. On nearly every major news show, interview subjects calling for more gun control far outnumber those who advocate making guns more readily available. This bias in favor of gun control ignores evidence that suggests that more firearms restrictions will make the United States a more dangerous place.

To investigate television coverage [of gun issues], I collected stories reported on the evening news broadcasts and morning news shows on the three major networks (ABC, CBS, and NBC) during 2001. In 2001 there were several segments discussing the increase in gun sales after September 11, and a couple of these shows went so far as to give the desire for self-defense as a reason. But despite slightly over 190,000 words of coverage on gun crimes, merely 580 words were devoted by one news broadcast to an armed off-duty police officer who helped stop a school shooting. None of the three networks mentioned any other defensive gun use—certainly not one by a civilian.

ABC's *Good Morning America* program is fairly typical of broadcasting in the way it treats gun stories. It unquestionably leads its competitors in terms of the sheer volume of stories it does on guns, with almost 77,000 words spent on stories discussing gun crimes. Guests supporting gun control included Rosie O'Donnell, Randy Graves [whose son was severely wounded during the April 20, 1999, shooting spree at Columbine High School], an academic from Emory University urging people to "remove the guns from the home," and Representative Carolyn McCarthy from New York, whose husband was killed in Colin Ferguson's 1993 [shooting] rampage on the Long Island Rail Road. Not one single guest provided an alternative viewpoint. Twelve segments covered the Santana High School shooting in Santee, California, where two students were killed [in 2001]. Eight segments examined the Williamsport, Pennsylvania, shooting, where one student was wounded. And four segments were devoted to an attack at a California Community College, where a student was caught before he could act out his plan.

Other topics on *Good Morning America* during 2001 included a September discussion of school shootings that had taken place during previous academic years, the second anniversary of the Columbine attack, a town meeting on school violence, a mother who shot her six-year-old son, celebrity shootings allegedly involving [actor] Robert Blake and rapper Sean "Puffy" Combs, Texas prison escapees who were committing crimes with guns, a former IRS employee who shot at the White House, and the murder of a Dekalb County, Georgia, sheriff.

If stories on lives lost by guns are interesting, why not interview a heroic youngster who saved lives with a gun?

ABC's other news program, *World News Tonight*, covered many of the same topics as well as a few others. Among the additional stories were two different shootings where a man killed someone at a plant and then committed suicide (in Indiana and Illinois), some general pieces on school shootings, and an examination of "Secret Service Techniques Used in Threat Assessment." Even a story about the mentally ill managed to raise the issue of crimes committed with guns.

Media's support for gun control

If I were a TV news director, I admit I would probably also cover many of these same stories. Yet, while a murder/suicide at a plant in Indiana or Illinois is interesting, does it really merit coverage on the national evening news? A mother who shoots her son is also important, and so is the murder of a Georgia sheriff. But surely at least one defensive gun story . . . would also be as newsworthy. Within just the randomly selected two-week period . . . a killer in Michigan was stopped from firing his gun at passing cars by a concealed permit holder. In other cases not covered on television news, multiple lives were saved—more lives than were lost in some of the stories that made the national news.

The imbalance of viewpoints on television news is even more difficult to explain than the choice of stories covered. Of the morning show hosts, only Katie Couric interviewed NRA president Charlton Heston (March 13). One interview with Charlton Heston by the *Today Show* doesn't balance extensive interviews with Rosie O'Donnell, Million Mom March founder Donna Dees-Thomases, multiple parents who had lost their children to gun violence, and an extensive discussion about how people should try to convince their neighbors not to own guns. Not one person, including Heston during his brief interview, suggested that gun control could increases crime. If stories on lives lost by guns are interesting, why not interview a heroic youngster who saved lives with a gun? If asking neighbors to stop owning guns makes for interesting television, it ought to be equally interesting to interview researchers whose work shows that increased gun ownership saves lives.

A challenging interviewer would ask gun control advocates about the strongest objections provided by their opponents.

The television media's support for more gun control in news reports is often quite explicit and frequently takes the form of lobbying. Take a segment on CBS's *Early Show:*

> *Diana Olick* (reporter): When shots rang out in the halls of Santana High last week, they fell, some say, on deaf ears in the halls of Congress. . . .
>
> *Representative Carolyn McCarthy:* I've had an awful lot of members say to me, "Carolyn, I wish I could vote with you. I can't." That's how powerful the NRA is.
>
> *Olick:* But the facts don't support the fear. In Election 2000, five new senators won their seats running on the gun issue. And according to the Million Mom Organization, five out of seven congressional candidates won with strong positions on gun control.
>
> *Ms. Donna Dees-Thomases* (Million Mom Organization): I believe that some of these elected officials, quite frankly, are just cowards. They are afraid of the gun lobby. But shame on them.
>
> *Olick:* . . . Representative Carolyn McCarthy says that in the next few months she'll introduce another bill trying once again to require background checks at gun shows. Such a bill did not pass in the last session. Julie.
>
> *Julie Chen* (anchor): All right. Thanks, Diana. Diana Olick on Capitol Hill. And just ahead, we'll hear from the mother of one of the victims of the Santana High shooting.

As the quotes at the beginning of this section also indicate, anchors and reporters always assume that more gun control is the answer.

Their bias shows up in the questioning of guests. A challenging interviewer would ask gun control advocates about the strongest objections provided by their opponents. Opponents of controls should of course face the same critical questioning. Instead, gun control advocates are frequently pushed to support more restrictions than they are currently advocating. All too typical was Bryant Gumbel's questioning of Senator John McCain when Gumbel asked what McCain would do if his current gun control efforts on gun show regulations failed. Gumbel didn't ask whether McCain would reconsider his support of control. Instead, Gumbel wanted to know "Could you see your position reaching the point where you might support registration; where you might support longer waiting periods?"

Television anchors encourage gun control advocates in ways one could never imagine them treating gun control opponents. Katie Couric worried aloud about the charges of hypocrisy Rosie O'Donnell faced when her bodyguards applied for concealed handgun permits: "And you were demonized by the people who believe in the right to carry guns."

However, there is a notable exception to all this one-sided coverage on the television news. I concentrated on the major networks simply because they have by far the largest audiences, but since the late 1990s the Fox News Channel has been providing an alternative approach. Even though Fox provides extensive live coverage of bad events involving guns, at least several news stories during 2001 and the first half of 2002 have explicitly discussed defensive gun use by citizens.

Whatever the motivation for this imbalance by the networks, the constant bombardment of bad news about guns has an impact on people's views.

13

Negative Media Bias Benefits Gun Rights Activists

Bernie DeGroat

Bernie DeGroat is the media relations officer at the University of Michigan Business School.

Gun rights advocates often blame the media for antigun bias. Ironically, this bias actually helps the progun National Rifle Association (NRA). The often extremely negative media coverage of the NRA provokes gun rights sympathizers to swell the ranks of the organization. The NRA, in turn, uses membership funds to support a powerful lobbying arm that fights gun control and successfully pushes progun legislation in state and federal capitals. In this case, media bias actually helps the very cause it is trying to hurt.

The recent onslaught of unfavorable media coverage given to gun rights advocates and the National Rifle Association (NRA) [in 1999] is actually a boon to NRA membership and will help increase its influence, says a University of Michigan researcher.

"The more negative media coverage the NRA receives, the larger its membership grows," says Brian A. Patrick, who recently earned a doctorate in communication at the U-M. "In light of intense negative coverage received by the NRA as a result of the recent school shootings in Colorado and Georgia, membership in the NRA will increase markedly for a time and will continue to trend upward as it has in the past 30 years.

"In essence, the NRA has institutionalized around bad press, using it as a rallying point in mobilizing members."

In an analysis of nearly 1,500 articles in what Patrick calls the "elite" press—*New York Times, Washington Post, Los Angeles Times, Wall Street Journal* and *Christian Science Monitor*—from 1990 until 1998, Patrick compared the coverage of the NRA with that of the NAACP [National Association for the Advancement of Colored People], American Civil Liberties Union (ACLU), American Association of Retired Persons (AARP) and Handgun Control Inc. (HCI).

He found that although the NRA garnered much more negative coverage than the other four interest groups along 16 objectively defined measures, the gun rights group increased its membership by more than 1 million to a high of 3.6 million during this time. Currently, membership is roughly 3 million with a core of about 500,000 life members.

Bad press rallies gun owners

Patrick's research shows a strong correlation between NRA membership and the number of negative editorials and op-ed articles. In other words, the greater the number of unfavorable editorials and op-eds about guns and the NRA in the "elite" press, the larger the increase in new NRA members.

"This should not be interpreted as meaning that the average hog farmer in Iowa happens to read a strident anti-NRA editorial over brunch while browsing the Sunday *New York Times* and the next day joins the NRA," Patrick says. "The frequency of editorials should be regarded as representative of negative NRA media coverage in general. A more reasonable scenario would be that the hog farmer is exposed to waves of gun-related coverage emanating from national news sources."

According to Patrick, 87 percent of editorials and op-eds covering the NRA are negative, while 52 percent of those on the NAACP, ACLU, AARP and HCI, collectively, are unfavorable. The editorial treatment of the NRA relative to other interest groups, he says, is due in large part to policy positions of editors, whose commentaries contain an unrestrained tone and semantics, "the likes of which are seldom directed at non-NRA groups."

In straight news coverage, Patrick found that the NRA averages little more than a paragraph of direct quotes or attributed viewpoints per article, compared with about three for the other interest groups in the study. Negative verbs of attribution, such as "claims," "contends," "asserts" and "argues"—rather than the more neutral "says" or "said"—also are used more often for NRA sources than for other sources.

"The more negative media coverage the NRA receives, the larger its membership grows."

"What this appears to do is to qualify NRA positions as tentative while representing the opinions of other sources as undisputed fact," Patrick says.

His research also shows that less than 20 percent of NRA officials quoted are identified with their proper organizational titles, compared with about 73 percent and 64 percent of NAACP and HCI sources, respectively, and nearly half of the sources for the ACLU and AARP. Mostly, NRA sources are referred to as "lobbyists" and are, more often than other interest groups, portrayed as having negative or unsympathetic personality traits, Patrick says.

Mocked in news coverage

Moreover, compared with other interest groups, the NRA is regularly mocked or satirized in news coverage and belittled with a greater number of joke headlines, he says. About 27 percent of the headlines for NRA stories since 1990 have used a joke or pun—more than twice the rate for any of the other interest groups.

Examples include: "The gun lobby, over a barrel," "NRA way off target," "Faltering NRA finds itself under the gun," "Have gun, will shoot," "NRA, in crosshairs of critics, fires fresh volley of words," and "Did NRA shoot itself in the foot?"

In addition, compared to other interest groups, the NRA is much less likely to attract media attention for what Patrick calls "pseudo-events"—news conferences, special events, demonstrations, reports, news releases, etc. Less than 7 percent of NRA coverage consists of these types of events, while such coverage ranges from about 29 percent to 43 percent for each of the other groups in the study.

The NRA is regularly mocked or satirized in news coverage and belittled with a . . . number of joke headlines.

Further, the NRA is more than twice as likely as the other groups to be described as a "lobby" or "special interest group"—terms that tend to have negative and anti-democratic connotations, Patrick says. Other groups are more likely to be referred to with more positive labels, such as an "advocacy group" or "citizen group."

Finally, only about 6 percent of NRA coverage includes photos of NRA officials or events, compared with 27 percent for the NAACP, ACLU, AARP and HCI, combined, Patrick says.

"In all, the NRA is indeed treated much differently than the other groups," he says. "And these differences are systematic, meaning they persist over time, across media sources and for many content categories across all article types. All this is not to say there is no fair coverage of the NRA or even that fair coverage is rare. On the whole, though, the numbers and proportions reported for the content categories speak for themselves.

"But since NRA communication strategies are measurably premised upon 'conflict' and 'media bias' themes, it may prove that negative press coverage, whether it is caused by elite journalists, cultural or class bias, whether actual or alleged, is an indispensable mobilizing tool of the NRA, providing fuel for activism, membership increase, fund raising and single-issue voting."

Organizations to Contact

The editors have compiled the following list of organizations concerned with issues debated in this book. The descriptions are derived from materials provided by the organizations. All have publications or information available for interested readers. The list was compiled on the date of publication of the present volume; the information provided here may change. Be aware that many organizations take several weeks or longer to respond to inquiries, so allow as much time as possible.

Accuracy in Media
4455 Connecticut Ave. NW, Suite 330, Washington, DC 20008
(202) 364-4401 • fax: (202) 364-4098
e-mail: ar1@aim.org • Web site: www.aim.org

Accuracy in Media is a nonprofit citizens' watchdog of the news media. It critiques liberal news stories and offers the conservative viewpoint on important issues that it believes have received slanted coverage.

American Library Association (ALA)
50 E. Huron, Chicago, IL 60611
(800) 545-2433 • fax: (312) 440-9374
e-mail: ala@ala.org • Web site: www.ala.org

The ALA is the oldest and largest library association in the world. It works to protect intellectual freedom and to promote high-quality library and information services. The ALA publishes the *Newsletter on Intellectual Freedom*, pamphlets, articles, posters, and an annually updated Banned Books Week Resource Kit.

Cato Institute
1000 Massachusetts Ave. NW, Washington, DC 20001-5403
(202) 842-0200 • fax: (202) 842-3490
e-mail: jblock@cato.org • Web site: www.cato.org

The Cato Institute is a nonprofit libertarian public policy research foundation headquartered in Washington, D.C. The Cato Institute seeks to broaden the parameters of public policy debate to allow consideration of the traditional American principles of limited government, individual liberty, free markets, and peace. The institute researches issues in the media and provides commentary for magazine, newspaper, and news show editorials.

Center for American Progress
805 Fifteenth St. NW, Suite 400, Washington, DC 20005
(202) 682-1611
e-mail: kcooper@amprog.org • Web site: www.centerforamericanprogress.org

The Center for American Progress is a research and educational institute dedicated to promoting progressive viewpoints on issues such as media bias, national security, the economy, and the environment. Their daily publication

Progress Report, available by e-mail, analyzes the media and questions viewpoints perceived to be biased toward conservative policies in the news.

Center for Investigative Reporting (CIR)
500 Howard St., Suite 206, San Francisco, CA 94105-3000
(415) 543-1200 • fax: (415) 543-8311
e-mail: cir@igc.org • Web site: www.muckraker.org

The CIR is a nonprofit news organization composed of journalists dedicated to encouraging investigative reporting. It conducts investigations, offers consulting services to news and special-interest organizations, and conducts workshops and seminars for investigative journalists. Its publications include the seasonal magazine *Muckraker* and the *Investigative Handbook*.

Center for Media and Public Affairs (CMPA)
2100 L St. NW, Suite 300, Washington, DC 20037
(202) 223-2942
e-mail: mail@cmpa.com • Web site: www.cmpa.com

The CMPA is a nonpartisan research and educational organization that conducts scientific studies of the news and entertainment media. Its continuing analysis and tabulation of late night political jokes provides a lighter look at major news makers. The CMPA is one of the few groups to study the important role the media play in communicating information about health risks and scientific issues.

Centre for Research on Globalisation (CRG)
RR #2, Shanty Bay, ON L0L2L0 Canada
(888) 713-8500 (United States and Canada)
e-mail: editor@globalresearch.ca • Web site: www.globalresearch.ca

The CRG is a Canadian-based group of progressive writers, scholars, and activists committed to curbing the tide of globalization. The CRG creates news articles, commentary, background research, and analysis on a broad range of issues, focusing on the interrelationship between social, economic, strategic, geopolitical, and environmental processes. The organization also publishes the quarterly magazine *Global Watch*.

Chilling Effects Clearinghouse
454 Shotwell St., San Francisco, CA 94110-1914
(415) 436-9333 • fax: (415) 436-9993
e-mail: questions@chillingeffects.org • Web site: www.chillingeffects.org

Chilling Effects aims to help people understand the protections that the First Amendment and intellectual property laws give to them concerning online publishing activities. Chilling Effects encourages respect for intellectual property law while frowning on its misuse to "chill" legitimate activity.

Democratic Underground (DU)
PO Box 53350, Washington, DC 20009
e-mail: mail@democraticunderground.com
Web site: www.democraticunderground.com

The DU was founded on Inauguration Day, January 20, 2001, to protest the questionable circumstances that allowed George W. Bush to become president. The organization provides resources for the exchange and dissemination of liberal and progressive ideas throughout the media. The DU has become one of the premier left-wing Web sites on the Internet, publishing original content six days a week and hosting one of the Web's most active left-wing discussion boards.

Fairness and Accuracy in the Media (FAIR)
112 W. Twenty-seventh St., New York, NY 10001
(212) 633-6700 • fax: (212) 727-7668
e-mail: fair@fair.org. • Web site: www.fair.org

FAIR is a national media watch group that documents media bias and censorship. FAIR advocates greater diversity in the press and scrutinizes media practices that marginalize public interest, minority, and dissenting viewpoints. FAIR publishes a bimonthly magazine, *Extra!*, which analyzes media treatment of important issues and points out perceived conservative bias.

Freedom Forum Media Studies Center
580 Madison Ave., New York, NY 10022
(212) 317-6500
e-mail: mfitzsi@mediastudies.org • Web site: www.freedomforum.org

The center is a research organization dedicated to studying the media and educating the public about their influence on society. It publishes numerous conference reports and papers, including *The Media and Women* and the biannual *Media Studies Journal.*

Information Clearing House (ICH)
PO Box 365, Imperial Beach, CA 91933
e-mail: tom@informationclearinghouse.info
Web site: www.informationclearinghouse.info

The ICH is an independent media source for unreported (or underreported) news from around the globe. The ICH's mission is to correct what it believes are the distorted perceptions provided by commercial media. Subscribers can receive a daily e-mail digest that presents the group's viewpoint on the headlines.

Media Research Center (MRC)
325 S. Patrick St., Alexandria, VA 22314
(800) 672-1423 • fax: (703) 683-9736
e-mail: mrc@mediaresearch.org • Web site: www.MediaResearch.org

The mission of the MRC is to bring a conservative viewpoint to the news media. MRC's mission is to prove—through scientific research—that liberal bias in the media exists and to neutralize the impact of this professed bias on the American political scene. The MRC publishes press releases, special reports, and daily e-mail alerts to cover perceived bias in news reporting.

Mediascope
100 Universal City Plaza, Bldg. 6159, Universal City, CA 91608
(818) 733-3180 • fax: (818) 733-3181
e-mail: facts@mediascope.org • Web site: www.mediascope.org

Mediascope is a national, nonprofit research and policy organization working to encourage responsible portrayals in film, television, the Internet, video games, music, and advertising. The organization addresses a variety of topics, including substance use, prevention of school violence and bullying, childhood obesity, media ratings, children's television, media violence, and artists' rights and responsibilities. The group publishes a quarterly newsletter, available by e-mail, and offers books, briefs, and other publications concerning what it perceives to be irresponsible behavior in the media.

Media Whores Online (MWO)
e-mail: mwo@mediawhoresonline.com
Web site: www.mediawhoresonline.com

MWO is an aggressively left-wing site that exposes what it believes are the foibles of right-wing journalists and media stars. Using unrestrained language and humor, MWO takes journalists to task for laziness and for reprinting conservative viewpoints with little investigation into the factual accuracy of the story.

National Association of Black Journalists (NABJ)
8701-A Adelphi Rd., Adelphi, MD 20783-1716
(301) 445-7100 • fax: (301) 445-7101
e-mail: nabj@nabj.org • Web site: www.nabj.org

Founded in 1975, the NABJ serves to strengthen ties among African American journalists, promote diversity in newsrooms, and honor the achievements of black journalists. It publishes the *NABJ Journal* ten times a year.

National Coalition Against Censorship
275 Seventh Ave., New York, NY 10001
(212) 807-6222 • fax: (212) 807-6245
e-mail: ncac@ncac.org • Web site: www.ncac.org

The coalition opposes censorship in any form, believing it to be against the First Amendment right to freedom of speech. It works to educate the public about the dangers of censorship, including censorship of violence on television and in movies and music. The coalition publishes *Censorship News* five times a year.

Take Back the Media
1072 Casitas Pass Rd., #125, Carpinteria, CA 93013
e-mail: info@takebackthemedia.com • Web site:
www.takebackthemedia.com

Take Back the Media is a cooperative project by progressive American citizens dismayed at what they see as progovernment, procorporate bias shown by American media. In addition, they advocate using economic boycotts and other nonviolent action to bring back responsibility to the corporate media.

TomPaine.com
PO Box 53303, Washington, DC 20009
e-mail: editor@tompaine.com • Web site: www.tompaine.com

TomPaine.com is a public-interest journal inspired by the great eighteenth-century patriot Thomas Paine, author of *Common Sense* and *The Rights of Man*. TomPaine.com seeks to enrich the national debate on controversial public issues by featuring the ideas, opinions, and analyses too often overlooked by the mainstream media.

Bibliography

Books

Eric Alterman	*Sound and Fury: The Making of the Punditocracy.* Ithaca, NY: Cornell University Press, 1999.
Eric Alterman	*What Liberal Media?* New York: Basic Books, 2003.
Sidney Blumenthal	*The Clinton Wars.* New York: Farrar, Straus and Giroux, 2003.
L. Brent Bozell and Brent H. Baker, eds.	*And That's the Way It Isn't: A Reference Guide to Media Bias.* Alexandria, VA: Media Research Center, 1990.
David Brock	*Blinded by the Right: The Conscience of an Ex-Conservative.* New York: Crown, 2002.
Noam Chomsky	*Media Control: The Spectacular Achievements of Propaganda.* Open Media Pamphlet Series. New York: Seven Stories, 1997.
Noam Chomsky	*Propaganda and the Public Mind.* Cambridge, MA: South End, 2001.
Jeff Cohen	*Through the Media Looking Glass: Decoding Bias and Blather in the News.* Monroe, ME: Common Courage, 1995.
Joe Conason	*Big Lies: The Right-Wing Propaganda Machine and How It Distorts the Truth.* New York: Thomas Dunne, 2003.
Ann H. Coulter	*Slander: Liberal Lies About the American Right.* New York: Crown, 2002.
Sarah Eschholz	*Crime on Television—Issues in Criminal Justice.* Atlanta: Georgia State University, 2003.
Laura Flanders, ed.	*Real Majority, Media Minority: The Cost of Sidelining Women in Reporting.* Monroe, ME: Common Courage, 1997.
Al Franken	*Lies (and the Lying Liars Who Tell Them): A Fair and Balanced Look at the Right.* New York: Dutton, 2003.
Al Franken	*Rush Limbaugh Is a Big Fat Idiot and Other Observations.* New York: Delacorte, 1996.
Bernard Goldberg	*Bias: A CBS Insider Exposes How the Media Distort the News.* Washington, DC: Regnery, 2002.
Tim Graham	*Pattern of Deception: The Media's Role in the Clinton Presidency.* Alexandria, VA: Media Research Center, 1996.
Peter Hart	*The Oh Really? Factor: Unspinning Fox News Channel's Bill O'Reilly.* New York: Seven Stories, 2003.

Jim Hightower	*If the Gods Had Meant Us to Vote They Would Have Given Us Candidates.* New York: HarperCollins, 2000.
Molly Ivins	*Bushwhacked: Life in George W. Bush's America.* New York: Random House, 2003.
Carl Jensen	*Twenty Years of Censored News.* New York: Seven Stories, 1997.
Rush Limbaugh	*See, I Told You So.* New York: Pocket Books, 1993.
John R. Lott Jr.	*The Bias Against Guns.* Washington, DC: Regnery, 2003.
Robert W. McChesney	*Corporate Media and the Threat to Democracy.* Open Media Pamphlet Series. New York: Seven Stories, 1997.
Robert W. McChesney	*Rich Media, Poor Democracy: Communication Politics in Dubious Times.* Urbana: University of Illinois Press, 1999.
Robert W. McChesney and John Nichols	*Our Media, Not Theirs.* New York: Seven Stories, 2002.
Michael Moore	*Dude, Where's My Country?* New York: Warner Books, 2003.
David Niven	*Tilt? The Search for Media Bias.* Westport, CT: Praeger, 2002.
Peter Phillips	*Censored 2004: The Top 25 Censored Stories.* New York: Seven Stories, 2003.
Peter Phillips	*Censored 2003: The Top 25 Censored Stories.* New York: Seven Stories, 2002.
Peter Phillips	*Censored 2002: The Top 25 Censored Stories.* New York: Seven Stories, 2001.
Steve Rendall, Jim Naureckas, and Jeff Cohen	*The Way Things Aren't: Rush Limbaugh's Reign of Error: Over 100 Outrageously False and Foolish Statements from America's Most Powerful Radio and TV Commentator.* New York: New Press, 1995.

Periodicals

Robin Andersen	"That's Militainment! The Pentagon's Media-Friendly 'Reality' War," *Extra!*, May/June 2003.
Peter Beinart	"TRB from Washington: Media Bias," *New Republic*, April 14, 2003.
David W. Brady	"Spot the Difference," *Wall Street Journal*, November 12, 2003.
Eric Burns	"Segment Three: Surprising Conclusions About Political Bias in Media," *America's Intelligence Wire*, July 9, 2003.
Karen Charman	"Hazy Reporting: Missing the Big Picture on Bush's Environmental Assault," *Extra!*, December 2003.
John C. Cotey	"Bestseller Trampled Under Footnotes," *St. Petersburg Times*, August 26, 2002.

John Dicker

"Media Q&A: Our Bias, Ourselves: Navel Gazing with the Experts," *Colorado Springs Independent*, January 29, 2003.

Ernest Dumas

"So Who Needs the Media?" *Arkansas Times*, March 31, 2000.

Jonah Goldberg

"Big Dumb Lie: Journalists Who Insist There Is No Media Bias Problem Are Just Cutting Themselves Off from the American Public," *American Enterprise*, July/August 2003.

Ted Green

"News Media Bias," *Senior Reflections*, September 30, 2001.

David Hogberg

"HateRush.com," *American Spectator*, November 6, 2003.

Janine Jackson, Peter Hart, and Rachel Coen

"Fear & Favor 2002—the Third Annual Report: How Power Shapes the News," *Extra!*, March/April 2003.

Chaim Kupferberg

"The Propaganda Preparation for 9/11," *Global Outlook*, no. 3, June 13, 2002.

Steve Rendall and Tara Broughel

"Amplifying Officials, Squelching Dissent," *Extra!*, June 2003.

David Zupan

"Be Skeptical: Giant Corporations Wield Unprecedented Power over the Public Mind," *Eugene Weekly*, February 8, 2001.

Internet Sources

Bernie DeGroat

"Negative Media Coverage Benefits Gun Rights Supporters and NRA," University of Michigan, June 24, 1999. www.umich.edu/~newsinfo/Releases/1999/Jun99/r062499a.html.

Charles Donefer

"A Guide to Right-wing Conspiracies: We're Left, They're Wrong," *Johns Hopkins News-Letter*, April 5, 2002. www.jhunewsletter.com/vnews/display.v/ART/2002/04/05/3cad0968a4158?in_archive=1.

Tim Graham

"Peter's Peace Platoon," Media Research Center, March 18, 2003. www.mediaresearch.org/specialreports/2003/peter03182003.asp.

Rich Noyes

"A Summer of Skewed News: The Liberal Tilt in TV's Economic Reporting," Media Research Center, September 19, 2002. www2.mediaresearch.org/specialreports/2002/atm20020919.asp.

Danny Schechter

"Blogging the War Away," Z Magazine Online, July/August 2003. www.zmag.org/ZMagSite/Aug2003/schechter0803.html.

Index